DATE DUE

OE 19 '97			
JY 1 00			
FE 4 03			

CONFLICT AND PEACE IN THE HORN OF AFRICA

Conflict and Peace in the Horn of Africa

Federalism and its Alternatives

Edited by
PETER WOODWARD
and
MURRAY FORSYTH

Dartmouth

Aldershot • Brookfield USA • Singapore • Sydney

mited

Aldershot
Hants GU11 3HR
England

Dartmouth Publishing Company
Old Post Road
Brookfield
Vermont 05036
USA

British Library Cataloguing in Publication Data
Conflict and Peace in the Horn of Africa:
Federalism and Its Alternatives
  I. Woodward, Peter II. Forsyth, Murray
  320.963

Library of Congress Cataloging-in-Publication Data
Conflict and peace in the Horn of Arica / edited by Peter Woodward
  and Murray Forsyth.
        p.   cm.
    Includes bibliographical references.
    ISBN 1-85521-486-5 : $57.95 (U.S. : est.)
    1. Africa, Northeast–Politics and government–1974- 2. Africa,
Northeast. I. Woodward, Peter, 1944- . II. Forsyth, Murray
Greensmith.
    DT367.8.C65   1994
    963.07–dc20
                                                              94-11913
                                                                  CIP

ISBN 1 85521 486 5

Printed in Great Britain by Ipswich Book Co. Ltd., Ipswich, Suffolk

Table of Contents

Notes on the Contributors

Dr Hussein M Adam is a Somali national educated in Tanzania. He has published various works on Africa, and currently teaches at the College of the Holy Cross, Worcester, Massachusetts.

Dr Asfa Wossen Asserate is a consultant for African and Middle Eastern affairs, and Chairman of the Council for Civil Liberties in Ethiopia (CCLE).

Professor Christopher Clapham teaches at the University of Lancaster. He is the author of numerous works, including *Transformation and Continuity in Revolutionary Ethiopia*, Cambridge University Press, 1988.

Professor Lionel Cliffe teaches at the University of Leeds. He has written extensively on Africa, and edited (with Basil Davidson) *The Long Struggle of Eritrea for Independence and Constructive Peace*, Spokesman, 1988.

Martin Dent was a colonial administrator in Nigeria before teaching at the University of Keele and writing on Africa.

Professor Richard Greenfield has taught at a number of African universities, and his extensive writings include *A History of Ethiopia*, Faber, 1962.

Paul B Henze was a member of the American foreign service for many years, and later joined the Rand Corporation. His numerous publications include *The Horn of Africa*, Macmillan, 1991.

Dr Tesfatsion Medhanie is a Senior Research Fellow at the University of Bremen. He has written on Africa and the Soviet Union, including *Eritrea: Dynamics of a National Question*, B R Gruner, Amsterdam, 1986.

Professor Dr Heinrich Scholler teaches at the University of Munich and has written extensively on Ethiopia.

Dr Bairu Tafla is a Senior Research Fellow at the University of Hamburg and has written extensively on the history of Ethiopia.

Dr Peter Woodward teaches at the University of Reading. His publications on north-east Africa include *Sudan: the Unstable State*, Lynne Rienner, 1990. He is also the editor of *African Affairs*, the journal of the Royal African Society.

Preface

This collection of twelve essays, written by specialists both from the Horn of Africa itself and from countries outside Africa - the United Kingdom, Germany and the United States of America - investigates the prospects for peace, political stability, and economic progress in one of the most troubled and poorest areas of the world. The book grew out of a conference that was held at the University of Leicester shortly before Christmas 1990. It was a remarkable conference, bringing together representatives of a broad range of political groups and movements in the countries of the Horn, some of whom were bitterly opposed to one another and had never sat down together in the same room. The conference was sponsored jointly by the Centre for Federal Studies at Leicester, and the Council for Civil Liberties in Ethiopia (CCLE). It owed much to the inspiration and support of the Chairman of the CCLE, Dr Asfa Wossen Asserate, who first mooted the idea of a conference in an address he gave at the Royal Institute of International Affairs, London, in 1990.

The book is not, however, simply a reproduction of the papers presented at the conference. Events have moved rapidly in the Horn since then, and this has meant that some of the original papers have become irrelevant and unsuitable for publication, while others have had to be substantially revised and updated. Completely new papers have also been commissioned so as to ensure that the book gives a balanced treatment of the four main countries of the Horn - Ethiopia, Eritrea, Sudan and Somalia - as well as of the major issues.

An important theme that recurs in most of the essays is that of federalism. Several of the contributors argue that a federal, or at least a strongly regionalised system of government, could lay an important part in helping to bring internal peace to the countries of the Horn. Some go further and argue that federal links between the countries of the Horn should also be worked towards. The federal arrangement established between Ethiopia and Eritrea in 1952 is discussed because, despite its shortcomings and ultimate fate, it remains the most significant attempt to introduce an expressly federal structure into the area - and even its defects may be instructive.

Federalism is thus a major theme of the essays, though it is not the only one. The ultimate aim of the book is to provide a constructive discussion of the political and economic problems of an area of Africa whose plight receives much transient treatment in the media and all too often by policy-makers as well, but too little close and sustained attention.

The editors wish to express their thanks to Julie Cornish, of the Centre for Federal Studies at Leicester, for her invaluable work in preparing the manuscript of the book for publication.

Peter Woodward
Department of Politics
University of Reading

Murray Forsyth
Centre for Federal Studies
University of Leicester

1 Historical Background to the Conflicts in Ethiopia and the Prospect for Peace

BAIRU TAFLA

At present, Ethiopia is suffering from acute famine and the aftermath of war. Though the whole continent of Africa is likewise submerged in political and economic crises, the Ethiopian case is unparalleled in length of time and the complexity of the problems involved. The war raged for 30 years; more than 15 political factions took part in the struggle; the interests of foreign powers were intricately interwoven with the political fabric of the region. The tragedy of this reality is that no solution is in sight. The few negotiations that have ever been attempted failed to achieve anything, not even to agree to negotiate! Why? Is there no hope at all of bringing lasting peace to this troubled region?

These are some of the questions which have distressed, and are still troubling, the minds of those directly concerned, as well as of those who sympathize with the afflicted inhabitants. Each of the political factions believes that the best solution is that contained in its programme. In essence, these programmes seek to redress the political and economic injustice the people have been suffering; but there is no agreement on the way to achieve this common aim. Some political bodies insist that the regions in which they operate would be better off if, and when, they dissociate themselves from the existing Ethiopian state and attain independence, while others believe that far-reaching political and economic changes within the boundaries of the existing state will be good enough to satisfy all groups.

These are the predominant trends, but if we leave the statement at that, it might mislead one into thinking that the 15 or more movements can be reduced to two distinct groups. Such a conclusion would indeed be an oversimplification of the problem at hand. The fact is that there is little consensus between any two groups or factions on the method of achieving peace and justice in the future, a circumstance which only favours a continuation of the devastating war.

1

As a compromise, some scholars have recently propounded the hypothesis that Ethiopian history might provide a solution to the problem. It is argued that as the Ethiopian state had survived historically for so long, and is only now threatened with disintegration, then perhaps we might learn from history how to perpetuate the country's unity.

At least two Ethiopians (Professor Getatchew Haile and Dr Asfa Wossen Asserate) looked back into the history of their country and came up with the proposal that 'federation' might be a solution for the survival of Ethiopia in its present geo-political form[1]. The hypothesis as such is interesting and I suppose its various aspects will be widely debated among Africans as well as outsiders. What is gratifying about it is the fact that at long last educated people native to North-east Africa (including emigrés) have begun to sound out their opinions needed through publications and conferences. In fact, the year 1990 may be regarded as the birth of a number of peace initiatives in Europe and North America as well as in Ethiopia itself[2]. These initiatives are in their embryonic stage and most of them are characterized by partisanship, but they may trigger further developments on higher and more neutral levels.

I have mentioned earlier the new trend to turn to history for a solution to the incessant war in Ethiopia. Perusing and carefully analysing one's own history is, of course, instructive and at times inspiring. I have used the term 'carefully' not unintentionally, because there is the danger of grasping the wrong history. Factual and critical studies of Ethiopian history have not yet been produced for all periods and all aspects. There are a few good treatises on particular themes, but for the rest you have to depend on original sources and your own prudence. A great deal of pseudo-historical material has been produced by political organs (including the monarchical and military governments) for propaganda purposes. Their impact is nonetheless limited, as they are easily identifiable. More misleading are those written by amateurs and money-makers who possess neither the skill nor the interest to tap the evidence. They lean heavily on translations and secondary sources, and thereby perpetuate the blunders of others and make wrong assertions. If Ethiopians fall into this trap (and indeed a few have), their own society is to blame at least in part. In Ethiopian tradition, the study of history meant meddling in politics, a most undesirable pastime from the viewpoint of the rulers. Its prerequisite, namely the freedom of expression, was also absent. Some 80 years ago, an Ethiopian writer raised in a critical essay the question when the time would come when Ethiopians would be able to deal with their history as they wish[3], and, unfortunately, his question stands unanswered today. The same sullen legacy still prevails, and one can only hope at the moment that Ethiopians abroad may shed their inhibitions and begin to scrutinize their past.

History is more relevant to understanding than to solving current problems, for no event is exactly the same as another, and neither the requirements of a particular time nor the responses offered by contemporary authorities can be identical to subsequent ones. But each historical happening is inevitably related to a host of other events so that we are entitled to search into the distant past to find out affinities to prevailing developments and to draw lessons that may enable us to tackle current problems from the right perspective. Accordingly, I shall attempt to review briefly some aspects of the historical causes of the present conflicts in Ethiopia. Since the immediate causes of the various conflicts are presumably known to all of us, I should like to concentrate on the factors in the more remote part that have favoured conflict.

Origins of the Conflicts

It is a scarcely disputed fact that the Ethiopian state is constituted of heterogeneous political entities, languages, religions and ways of life. This is not a recent phenomenon, as some writers allege. Ethiopia has been a motley state throughout the last seven hundred or more years. Even the precursor societies of Askum and Lasta were by no means homogeneous. They were all brought together through the instrumentalities of force, and to a limited extent inheritance, at different times, and under different circumstances. They also warred against each other intermittently so that on the surface Ethiopian history looks like a mere record of conflicts. This happened because of a variety of recurrent factors and the lack of efforts on the part of those who had the responsibility for making permanent solutions.

The wars displayed in the historical records were not all regional or national conflicts, although in some cases the overlap was so extensive that it is rather difficult to determine their categories with precision. We may distinguish at least four types of wars in Ethiopian history: wars of expansion, wars of defence or retribution, religious wars, and wars of dissatisfaction. Let us review each of the old types of war briefly to see whether we can relate them to any or all of the more recent conflicts.

(a) The war of expansion, which was also known by the conquerors as the war of pacification[4], was the classical method of state building in Ethiopia as also elsewhere in the world. The stone inscriptions of Adulis, Matara and Aksum boast of conquests of dozens of peoples who had their own political institutions on both sides of the Red Sea. Some were even removed from their home region and resettled elsewhere.[5] Most of these peoples were assimilated into the dominant society in the course of the subsequent centuries. But the same process continued as the political centre moved further south to the central highlands and as new peoples migrated into its areas of influence.

The Christian Kingdom had a political centre which was forced to move for various reasons from Askum to Lasta, and then to Shewa, Tana-Gondac and back to Tegray and Shewa respectively; but its boundaries were elastic and expanded or contracted depending on the military talent of the leadership. This very phenomenon required an intermittent war of expansion, particularly on the regions close to the political centre. This was necessary for security and economic reasons. Hence, a series of conquests were launched between the fourteenth and seventeenth centuries against the Sultanates on the south-eastern escarpment and adjacent the Cushitic-speaking peoples of the Gibe region (e.g. Kafa, Konta, Janjero or Yama) and the state of Senaar in the Sudan[6].The expansion came to a climax in the late nineteenth century when Menilek II brought under his control all the regions which constitute southern Ethiopia today.

This operation gave Ethiopia its present form except in the north where Eritrea was added later under quite a different procedure, but it also enlarged

3

the magnitude of the problems Ethiopia had to tackle. Its political institutions were scarcely as elaborate and effective as its military organization and could, therefore, offer no better alternatives to the new subjects. Besides, the expansion was atrociously bloody in some regions and the administration that followed was oppressive and exploitative. Some of the political movements of today point to the history of this expansion to explain their existence; but there appears to be no evidence that they presume it to be the direct cause of their emergence.

(b) The wars of defence or retribution can be documented from the fourth century, when Askum ruined Meroe, to the twentieth century, when Ethiopia had to fight against European colonialism; but since they have scarcely any impact on the present conflicts (except in the case of the Ethio-Somalia boundary question) suffice it to mention that very few internal contentions have been linked to external invasions. Desertions and unco-operativeness were restricted to individuals, as in the cases of Dejjazmatch Kasa Mertcha in 1867-68, Ras Wolde-Mika'el in 1876, Negus Menilek in 1889 and Dejjazmatch Haile Selassie in 1936. The peoples usually laid their disputes aside to resist foreign invasions, and this was particularly the case in the Egyptian-Ethiopian war of 1875-76 and the Italo-Ethiopian wars of 1895-96 and 1935-36. In view of this tradition and in view of the absence of substantial evidence, the accusation that the present popular political movements are instrumental to foreign elements is hardly justifiable.

(c) Religious wars, too, can be traced in Ethiopian history to a certain extent. Religious bigotry was not a typical attribute of Ethiopian society and, hence we do not find records of extraordinary religious conflicts comparable to those found in Middle Eastern and European history. The purge launched by Zar'a Ya'eqob (1434-67) against the followers of the indigenous religions[7], the conflict[8] between the followers of the Ethiopian Orthodox Church and the Roman Catholic Church under Susenyos (1607-32), and the brief attempt of Yohannes IV (1872-89) to christianize[9] the Muslims of Wallo, are the major instances of 'pure' religious wars recorded in Ethiopian history, but religion was also the undertone of the wars which raged for centuries between the Christian Kingdom, the Muslim Sultanates and the Beta Esra'el (commonly known as the Falasha) of Semen, whose primary motives were political domination and economic exploitation. The leaders on either side used religion to arouse feelings and rally the support of the peoples at the outbreak of the war, but did not pursue a policy of religious suppression after victory. A marginal case is that of Imam Ahmed Muhammed el-Ghazi whose war may be equated with external invasion anyway. However, I know of no contemporary political movement that has attempted to employ the instrumentality of religion to rally the support of the people. The allegation that some political fronts are organised on religious grounds is apparently based on numerical evidence for which other factors can equally well account.

(d) Finally, we have a series of wars in Ethiopian history which are collectively referred to by various writers as civil war, internecine war, tribal war, ethno-religious conflicts, etc. They greatly varied in motives, frequency, degree of intensity, and persistence. The responses of the 'central' government also varied accordingly depending on the strength and prudence of the rulers. Among the outstanding causes were succession to the throne, rancour of

4

offended individual notables, rivalry of political aspirants, and popular reaction to oppression. The last point should fix our attention, as it contains components most relevant to the question under consideration.

The Ethiopian political system has been traditionally autocratic. The kernel of the system was the person of the sovereign the nature of whose powers is described by many a writer. From among the Ethiopian writers, the most explicit description is given by a lifelong official and monarchist, Blattengeta Mahteme Selassie:

'The power of the Ethiopian King of Kings over his effective dominion has been extensive and unlimited. He is concerned with all temporal and spiritual matters. With his lofty prerogatives, he can appoint, dismiss, give, deny, imprison, release, mutilate, execute or pardon, and so forth. The people – from the eldest to the youngest – accept his order with pleasure and without reservation, believing that he is the representative of God. I do not believe there is any other country where the Negus is so respected and loved as in Ethiopia. Even his name is dreaded. I do not think there is anyone – however rich or brave – who proceeds further when demanded to stop in the name of the Negus, or who fails to appear at an appointment to which he has sworn "by the death of the Negus", or who does not honour an agreement undertaken (in his name). The key phrase of oath in the ceremony of revered matrimony, too, consists of "... by the death of the Negus". As an example of the awe for the word of the Negus in our country, Ethiopia, one may cite the proverb that 'When demanded in the name of the Negus, not only the person but the running water stops.'"[10]

These prerogatives were invariably assumed by the rulers, some of whom, in fact, misused them frequently. The peoples were often impressed by the might and splendour of the despot, but scarcely found pleasure in obeying his commands. Not all the monarchs were able administrators nor were their appointees more judicious. The chronicles are, therefore, filled with accounts of popular uprisings not only in the newly conquered regions but also in the traditional communities from which the rulers themselves originated. Occasionally, there were a number of such uprisings at a time, but there was no co-ordination among them. Usually, these insurrections were crushed through military means; but the sensible rulers inhibited further rebellions by appointing, in consultation with the elders, governors of the peoples' preference, by reducing taxes, by the reinstitution of traditional laws and practices, and by providing a kind of autonomy. Such provisions were nevertheless temporary, as the next ruler or governor was not bound by the contracts of his predecessor. A new ruler, therefore, meant fear and insecurity to the people.

The Ethiopian political tradition concentrated on personality cult and failed to develop permanent political and judicial institutions to which the peoples could orient themselves. The institution of judicial administration was indeed one of the oldest components of Ethiopian culture, but it was rendered subservient to the political organ in the course of time. The head of state, the chief executive, the commander-in-chief of the military and the chief justice was one and the same person, and his provincial governors were nothing but miniatures of their master. On the event of the sovereign's death the rule of law broke down, though in most cases only temporarily. Even in the period of

5

relative peace and stability, the spirit of law was practically inert. As early as the late nineteenth century, an Ethiopian writer dared to remark that 'In Ethiopia a law is legislated but not put into practice'.[11] Even the customary laws of the people were often violated or replaced by alien and inequitable laws. In the absence of an institution through which the peoples' complaints could be voiced [12], uprisings were usually the means employed to express their discontent. Such uprisings cropped up as late as the 1960's, but they were unco-ordinated and scarcely articulate, and they could, therefore, not bring about the desired changes. The same problems and reactions have inevitably accentuated in the second half of the present century as a result of western education, foreign ideology and international communication. At long last, the fragmented demands for justice and democracy synthesized into a universal issue. But the approach to justice and democracy has proved a disastrous point of dissension.

In the same way that the Ethiopian political tradition bestowed power and authority upon a single personality, so it tended to favour centralism. It failed to recognise the significance of local or regional government as parts of a serviceable political system. The rulers obviously confused administrative plurality with disintegration and anarchy. The aversion to it became stronger after the eighteenth century when secession menaced the Empire. By refusing to pay tribute to the King of Kings and by defeating the imperial army, Shewa became the first autonomous region to secede around 1730 and could not fully be reintegrated until 1889. Then followed the chaotic period known as the Era of the Princes (c. 1769-1855) when the power of the monarchy waned to its lowest ebb and the provincial lords warred against one another. The Empire could be saved from complete dismemberment only by the rise of four successive monarchs who believed in the revival and perpetuation of the Christian Kingdom of Ethiopia.

In modern times, almost all the rulers favoured centralism. Tewodros II preferred external candidates to local ones for gubernatorial offices, though he turned to the latter at critical moments; Menilek II respected local government in the early years of his reign, but he attempted later to undermine regional autonomy. Haile Selassie I, who admired seventeenth century French absolutism, systematically removed all traditional regional or local prerogatives and perfected centralism. In fact, he removed most of the traditional territorial boundaries and clustered different political units (some of which were old rivals) into arbitrary provinces. His determination to dismantle the Eritrean federal system can be regarded as a part of this line of thinking which equated unity with uniformity. His prime minister, Aklilu Habte-Wold, lauded him on various public occasions as the initiator of 'rule through proxy' versus the 'hereditary system of local government'. But this innovation was devoid of efficiency, equity and distribution of wealth, and hence it caused everywhere intense dissatisfaction in the comprehensive sense of the term: 'Unhappiness caused by the failure of one's hopes, desires, or expectations'.The loss of hope is perhaps the most important element in the outbreak of the political commotion in Ethiopia. None of the movements took arms before trying to solve the problems through peaceful means. The Eritreans accepted the compromise settlement of their political future in 1952 with the hope that they might continue to enjoy at least the few democratic rights they had. There

6

was no acrimony or hostility for at least the first half dozen or so years, although the imperial government violated the federal constitution from the very beginning. In fact, some of the ardent opponents of association with Ethiopia had accepted offices. Protests became loud only when the systematic dismantling of the federal structure was well advanced, and hostilities broke out openly after the constitution was totally revoked. Similarly, the numerous protests of the intellectuals and students of the 1960's and early 70's were based on the hope that reforms could be brought about without bloodshed. The hopes and expectations of the same people were dashed not only by the adamant attitude of the imperial government, but also by the military government which they supported in its seizure of power.

Conclusions and Prospects

The existing conflicts in Ethiopia are evidently the results of historical problems which were never dealt with effectively. While the Ethiopian political organ succeeded in bring about a large state, it failed to develop a mechanism by which that state could be maintained permanently. It relied entirely on its military power to rule the people. Its administrative politics have been crude and harsh, and the rule of law has been practically neglected. The administrative apparatus has, through inefficiency and corruption, as well as through the use of excessive force, alienated the population. Armed uprisings became, as a matter of course, the popular reactions to these invariable problems. In the course of time, a huge gap appeared which had repercussions on internal relations; namely, a mutual lack of confidence. From the viewpoint of the people, both the old regime and the one that replaced it were total failures which could not be tolerated in any way. Conversely, from the point of view of these two regimes, all political movements were sinister instruments of foreign elements designed to disintegrate the country. This crisis of trust can by no means be solved easily. A change of attitude on the part of all groups concerned is a prerequisite for peace in Ethiopia.

If, and when, circumstances allow negotiation of all parties at the round table (and this is the most trustworthy course to peace), federalism or, to be precise, the equitable distribution of political power, may be worth considering as a permanent solution for the troubled region. However plausible this may sound it is by no means without difficulty. Federalism has had an unfortunate history in the region and is regarded in some quarters as repulsive. The Eritrean-Ethiopian Federation, which set an ominous precedent, had two inherent problems: it was imposed from outside and was tolerated by both Eritrea and Ethiopia on the basis that 'half a loaf is better than nothing'. It was also a marriage between two incompatible beings - the giant and the dwarf, the strong and the weak, the rich and the poor, the autocratic and the democratic. This mistake must by all means be avoided in the future. If we accept the fact that federation by definition necessarily implies equality of the involved entities, then it is difficult to speak of federation between Ethiopia and Eritrea, for example, without first recognizing the sovereignty of the latter. An alternative would be to make a clear distinction between Ethiopia and its

7

modern components. This requires a recognition of historical realities which may be difficult for some pollyannas. It is a fact that there is no core to be identified as Ethiopia. Ethiopia is a political superstructure embracing a number of political entities brought together in the course of a long history. It is these entities that will constitute the membership of a federation, and not the fabric that one attempts to create on the basis of language or some other political expediency. Spelling out the number and size of those political units lie beyond the scope of this paper, but it should be noted that the guarantee for permanent peace and stability even under a federal system lies in decisions based on the explicit will of the people.

---

1   Cf Getatchew Haile, 'What Form Of Government Should Ethiopia Have: Lessons From History' - a paper submitted to the 'Forum for Democracy in Ethiopia' on 2 February 1990 (Collegeville, Minnesota, January 1990); Asfa Wossen Asserate, 'Federalism - Ethiopia's Only Hope' - lecture given at the Royal Institute for International Affairs, London, on 7th February 1990.

2   Among the well known initiatives that followed the attempts of ex-President Carter and that of the Italian Government were the multi-factional conference held at Toronto, Canada, in May 1990 and the peace call of the religious leaders in Ethiopia issued in July. Cf *Horn Of Africa Bulletin* (Uppsala, vol 2 no 6 1990) 14. The Evangelische Akademie, Muhlheim (Germany), sponsored a forum on 21-23 September in which several of the political movements as well as a representative of the current Ethiopian government participated, while 'Eritreans for Peace' organised at least two conferences in Baltimore and London respectively in November.

3   Cf Gabra Heywat Bakadan, *Ate Menilekenna Ityopeya* (= 'Emperor Menilek and Ethiopia') = *Berhan Yekhun* (Asmara 1912) 336.

4   The term the chroniclers usually used to describe the expeditions of conquests was 'Oanna' which literally meant 'to   straighten up' and which figuratively signified 'to pacify, to develop, to civilise'. Cf Dasta Takla Wald, *Addis yamarena mazgaba qalat bakahnatenna bahagara sab qwanqwa tasafa* = A new dictionary of Amarena. Written in accordance with the parlance of the clergy and the peasants (Addis Ababa 1962 A.Mis. = 1969-70).

5   See the inscriptions reproduced in Enno Littmann (ed),*Sabaische, Griechische and Altabessinische Inschriften* = Deutsche Aksum-Expedition IV (1913) 4-12, 24 f, 28 f; Cf Sergew Hable Sellassie, *Ancient and Medieval Ethiopian History* to 1270 (Addis Ababa 1972) 63 f. None of the peoples listed in these inscriptions as being subjugated by the sovereigns have survived as an ethnic entity, but historians are of the opinion that they formed the substratum of the Tegrenna and Amarenna speaking peoples.

6   The royal chronicles and hagiographies published by Jules Perruchon, Carlo Conti Rossini, William L Conzelman, Esteves Pereira, Ignazio Guidi and others contain testimonies on these expeditions. The best analytical study on the first half of the mentioned period has been the work of Taddesse Tamerat, *Church and State in Ethiopia 1270-1527* (London 1972).

7   Cf Jules Perruchon (ed), *Les Chroniques de Zar'a Ya'eqob et de Ba'eda Maryam* (Paris 1893) 4-8.

8   FM Esteves Pereira (ed), *Chronica de Susenyos, Rei de Ethiopia* (Lisbon 1892) 187-320.

9   Cf Maurice de Coppet (ed), *Chronique du regne de Menelik II - roi des rois d'Ethiopie* (Paris 1930-31) 156 f; Bairu Tafla (ed), Asma Giyorgis and his Work: *History of the Galla and the Kingdom of Sawa* = Athiopistische Forschungen 18 (Stuttgart 1987) 687-97.

10 Mahtama Sellase, *Zekra Nagar* (Addis Ababa 1942 A.Mis. = 1949-50; 2nd ed. 1962 = 1969-70) 52 f.

11 Bairu Tafla, *Asma Giyorgis* (1987) 119.

12 In critical situations, the people could make use of direct appeal to the common sense of the head of state, but the effectiveness of this possibility was limited by geographical distances and intrigues of the ruling cliques. An example of the latter occurred in the seventeenth and eighteenth centuries, when the inhabitants of Tegray were denied entry to

the city of Gondar to present appeals. Instead, they were required to wave a piece of cloth and cry from the top of a mountain on the outskirts.

2 Future Relations between Ethiopia and Eritrea: Two Perspectives

A The Ethiopian Federation of 1952: an Obsolete Model or a Guide for the Future?

HEINRICH SCHOLLER

Before discussing the legal structure of the Ethiopian Federation of 1952 - the federation between Eritrea and Ethiopia - it is necessary to examine how far political and historical conditions favour the introduction or development of federal structures within Ethiopia, or between Ethiopia and other North African peoples. The success of such structures depends - and will depend - on the degree to which they are anchored in social and political reality, and not seen as an alien imposition.

In an earlier paper I made use of political anthropology to answer this question.[1] I would like here to take up again, and to develop, my earlier argument. I will then look at the main features of the 1952 federal structure.

The Social and Political Background

If we look into Ethiopian history we find egalitarian social elements linked directly with hierarchical elements of rule. Social structure and spiritual or mystical hierarchy have always been two factors which have permeated and determined state and society in Ethiopia. The pluralism of ethnic groups inhabiting the region can be seen as representing the 'horizontal' element in the history and culture of the country, while the dominance of the Amhara and Tigre in this community of peoples, with their spiritual-mystical superstructure, can be seen as the 'vertical' element. The vertical element corresponds more closely to the western model of unitary rule, while the horizontal one corresponds more closely to a federal model.

Historical myth has always been of great significance for Ethiopia, and the ruling Amhara and Tigre have known how to make use of it. The myth begins with King Solomon and the Queen of Sheba, continues with the legend of the priest-king John (Prester John), and ends in a certain sense with the vision of the re-arisen Emperor, who returns to purify the faith, to restore the Empire, and to initiate the world rule of Jerusalem. Revolutionary Ethiopia has added a new myth to this classic one, namely the myth of the 3000-year class struggle of the dispossessed Ethiopian peasant against feudal rule.

In the course of Ethiopian history the relationship of the horizontal and vertical elements has been subject to change. One important expression of the vertical element is the ideal of the Emperor as the 'King of Kings' *(Negusa Negest)*, which is connected with the idea of him as the conquering 'Lion of Judah'. This concept, however, allowed for the creation of a feudal-federal system of indirect rule which granted local cultural and socio-economic independence, so long as the contribution to the central power, the *Negusa Negest*, was duly paid. The idea that the Empire and the Negus are instruments of 'world peace' adds another vertical element to the societal pattern, one that was reinforced by pre- and post-Christian monotheism.

The vertical is also represented by the Ethiopian Church, which was very closely connected with the Emperor from the Ethiopian middle ages onwards. To the vertical belongs, too, the influence of Amharic as the state language, and the claim to leadership which Ethiopia has always made, even after the liberation of Africa.

The Ethiopian Church itself - in the medieval language *Ge'ez* - is absolutely hierarchical. The fact that within it the spiritual and temporal powers are represented and exercised by two different authorities - the Abuna and the Ichege - will not be analysed here, although it could be said to constitute a horizontal element in the hierarchical structure.

Popular paintings show the interaction of the secular and religious powers clearly, when they depict in the court of the Negus, the learned priest reading to him the Fetha Negast, the traditional lawbook based on canonic and Roman-Syrian law.

The horizontal element is provided by the plurality of peoples that occupy the region of Ethiopia. It expresses itself in the multiplicity of languages, and in the meeting together of the great religions - Christianity, Islam and Judaism - and their different socio-religious structures. Of particular significance are the three ethnic groupings and their differing conceptions of social and political order. These racial-ethnic groups can be roughly distinguished into Semitic, Cuchitic and Nilotic peoples. Alongside the Amharic, the Tigre, and other related Semitic languages, stand the Cuchitic languages. To them belong the Bega in Eritrea, the Agaw in the Danikil Desert, the Oromo groups and the Sidamo peoples in the west. The Nilotic or negroid tribes can be distinguished as a third group. They are concentrated on the western border of Ethiopia.

This multiplicity of peoples and this linguistic plurality is linked to completely different ways of thought about rule and empire. We find amongst the Oromo, but also amongst the Nuer, or Anuak, a form of segmentary or acephalic society, i.e. a strongly horizontal mode of politics.

11

The so-called Gadda-system is a kind of compromise between hierarchical and horizontal structures. Here there is a segmentary clan system, but at the same time a form of rule in which political and military functions are attached to certain age-groups, based always on a cycle of eight years. A man in his fifth cycle reaches his highest position in society, while the older generation withdraws from political life.

In Ethiopian history the now strongly 'amharised' Oromo have for centuries posed a threat to the Amharic Empire and Amharic rule. The 'heathen Galla' were conquered by force, Christianised and incorporated into the imperial union. The Oromo nobility linked itself with the Amharic royal house, while the destruction of Oromo culture through a feudal administration in the south went rapidly ahead. The leading officers of the Ethiopian army were predominantly of Oromo descent. In this way domesticated 'horizontal' elements were brought into the 'vertical' Amharic structure of rule. The Ethiopian Revolution, which brought the Derg, or military council to power, has also been called the revenge of the Oromo, because for a time the Oromo delegates held a majority in the Derg.

Another significant horizontal element lies in the fact that the Amhara did not found towns in the modern sense. The 'Katema' towns were really defence posts. The Negus moved continuously between them. Apart from the Gondar period, and then only temporarily, there was no capital city in Ethiopia until the founding of Addis Ababa at the end of the last century.

Finally, the traditional importance attached to 'right' and 'left' in society and state served to temper the hierarchical tendency. Not only was the court of the Negus organised on the basis of the complete equality of right and left - for example the law-giving body had 22 members on the left and on the right - but originally the next highest authority to the Negus, the Beht Wadad, was represented by two persons, one to the right and one to the left.

The historical blend of horizontal and vertical in Ethiopian society requires to be restructured in an adequate, modern constitution. Constitution does not mean a new foundation, but a putting together of what exists. How far this task was fulfilled by the federation between Ethiopia and Eritrea will now be examined.

Pre-history of the Federation of 1952

Eritrea became an Italian colony in 1900, after Italian forces had gradually conquered the country in the years following 1889. From 1900 until its liberation in 1942 Eritrea was administered as a colony by the Italian Colonial Ministry, under a Governor nominated by the Italian King. It was divided into seven administrative districts: Hamasein, Massawa, Assab, Akkeli Guzai, Serae, Keren and Barka, each under a provincial commissioner and his district officials, all of whom were Italians up until 1941. After its liberation by the British, Eritrea was governed by the latter. The commanding general bore the title 'Chief Administrator' and was subordinate to the Commander-in-Chief Middle East Land Forces. The four victorious allies established an investigating committee which was,

12

however, unable to come to a decision. As a result, the United Nations were given the following competence by Annexe XI, para. 3 of the Peace Treaty with Italy:

' If with respect to any of these territories the Four Powers are unable to agree upon their disposal within one year from the coming into force of the Treaty of Peace with Italy, the matter shall be referred to the General Assembly of the United Nations for a recommendation and the Four Powers agree to accept the recommendation and to take appropriate measures for giving effect to it.'

The administrative units were reduced to five, and the two largest, Keren and Agordat, were combined into the Western Province. The other provinces were Hamasein, Red Sea, Serae, and Akkeli Guzai.

The United Nations Commission for Eritrea concluded its work on 2 December 1950. The General Assembly, on the basis of the Commission's Report, decided that Eritrea should form an 'autonomous unit federated with Ethiopia under the sovereignty of the Ethiopian Crown'. A United Nations Commissioner was sent out with the task of drawing up a Constitution for Eritrea and presenting it to the General Assembly.

The first seven articles of the Resolution passed by the UN General Assembly on 2 December 1950 formed the so-called Federal Act. The draft Constitution was to be produced after discussions with Eritrean and Ethiopian officials, and after its ratification by the Emperor of Ethiopia, the Federal Act was to come into force. For a transitional period the British administration was to continue to exist. Furthermore, a representative assembly of Eritreans 'chosen by the people' was to be summoned. (The administration issued an Electoral Law and summoned the Assembly.) After some changes the draft Constitution was passed by the Eritrean Assembly on 10 July 1952. On 15 September 1952 the British administration transferred its functions to the Eritrean agencies and to the Ethiopian federal administration. By Proclamation No 124 of 11 September 1952, the Eritrean Constitution, with the Federal Act, was put into force in Negarit Gazeta. At this point the Federation of Eritrea with Ethiopia came into effect.

The UN Commissioner had stressed in his report (chapter 6), that there was a strong desire that the Constitution should be short and clear, and without unnecessary detail. Only the general constitutional principles were to be included, in order to leave further constitutional development open to practice. Organisational acts followed, namely:

1. The Administration of Justice Proclamation .
2. The Eritrean Functioning of Government Act.
3. The Eritrean Electoral Act.
4. The Eritrean Budget Act.
5. The Eritrean Audit Act.
6. The Eritrean Advisory Council Act.
7. The Eritrean Civil Service Act.

By Proclamation No 36, the British put into effect the Termination of Powers Act, which transferred authority and power to Eritrea and Ethiopia.

13

The Eritrean Constitution

The Constitution contained 99 articles and was divided into seven parts. Each of these seven parts was again divided in chapters and sections. The preamble took the form of a prayer.

In the first part are contained the general stipulations relating to the Federal Act. In chapter 1 of part one the status of Eritrea is described in terms of territory, legislation, the executive, and the judiciary, as well as the participation of Eritrean authorities in the federal power. This chapter concludes with citizenship and the rights of Eritrean and Ethiopian citizens.

The second chapter relates to the Emperor's legal position in Eritrea (Art. 10 to Art. 15), while the third chapter deals with the democratic governmental power in Eritrea (Art. 16 to Art. 21). This includes general stipulations about democratic government and the national flag (Art. 20 and 21). Chapter four then sets out a list of human rights and fundamental liberties, which partially reproduce or expand upon those contained in the Federal Act, for example: freedom and equality before the law, freedom of conscience and religion (Art. 26), an anti-discrimination rule (Art. 27), religious education and services, right to education (Art. 29 and Art. 31), work conditions and trade unions, as well as the guarantee of human rights and fundamental liberties (Art. 34). In chapter five, follow the special rights of the different ethnic groups in Eritrea in relation to prosperity, language, and personal status.

Part two deals with the Assembly, i.e. the Parliament, and is divided into the following chapters:

1. Election and composition of the Assembly
2. Sessions
3. The position of Members of Parliament
4. The Assembly's powers.

The executive is regulated in part three by three chapters, dealing with nomination and composition, executive power, and the administration.

Part four contains rules for the Advisory Council of Eritrea, and part six those for amendments to the constitution. Finally in part seven there are transitional provisions concerning the coming into force of the Constitution, and the continued effect of former law, continuation of obligations, and the guarantee of the continuation of contracts of employment.

The Federal Character of Ethiopia and Eritrea: General Provisions

The second article and part one of the Constitution contains the following basic norm:

'The territory of Eritrea, including the islands, is that of the former Italian colony of Eritrea.'

The statement that Eritrea is an 'autonomous unit federated with Ethiopia' (Art. 3) could be taken to denote a confederation consisting of the two independent states of Eritrea and Ethiopia, linked only by the Ethiopian Emperor in a personal union. This, however, was not the intention, and does not accord with the wording of Art. 3. The term 'autonomous unit' signifies not a sovereign state, but rather a politically organised unit linked federally with Ethiopia.

The phrase 'under the sovereignty of the Ethiopian Crown' does not imply a personal union, but rather that the Federation, not the autonomous unit, enjoys sovereignty.

In its subsequent provisions, the constitution never refers to the 'State of Eritrea', but only to the Government of Eritrea (Art. 4) and to the Assembly representing the Eritrean people (Art. 39). The Government of Eritrea is given legislative, administrative, and judicial powers (Art. 4), which are exercised independently of Ethiopia. Art. 5 lists the areas over which Eritrea can exercise legislative power: criminal law, civil law, trade law, public services, police, health services, education, public aid, employment law, resources, vocational law, agriculture and transport.

The first article is of special significance in this context. It speaks of the Eritrean people, which has accepted the Federal Act through its representatives. The federal power is symbolised in Eritrea by a representative of the Emperor (Art. 10 and Art. 11). Eritrea's Chief Executive is elected by the Eritrean Parliament. He or she is formally introduced into office by the Emperor (Art. 12). On the occasion of the opening and closing sessions of parliament, the Emperor's representative may give a speech from the throne and address issues of general importance to Eritrea and the Federation. In addition, the Emperor's representative has a right of veto in matters which concern the Federation. Exercise of the veto leads to a further debate and decision in parliament. Eritrean statutes are also promulgated by the Emperor's representative (Art. 15 and Art. 18). It is not clear if a simple or qualified majority is required to override the veto. On the whole these articles show the relatively strong, independent position of the autonomous unit of Eritrea, which is further enhanced by Art. 7, relating to the Imperial Federal Council. Eritrea's representatives in this Council are named by the Chief Executive, i.e. the Prime Minister of Eritrea with the Parliament's consent, and are only formally introduced into office by the Emperor. It is important to note that the number of Eritrean representatives equals that of the Ethiopian representatives.

When one asks the central question whether this federal model relates to the past or to the future, one must acknowledge its potential applicability to the future. However it is not clear what role a body such as the Federal Council ought to play in the future, in terms of advisory powers, legislative powers, and administration. Should it take part in federal legislation like the German Federal Council (Bundesrat), and if so, would equal representation of Ethiopia and Eritrea be feasible? One must further ask what should be the role of the representative of any future federation in Eritrea. Should that representative hold as strong a position as the Emperor's representative? Clearly, there must be a provision that his veto may be overruled by the Assembly (the Eritrean Parliament) by a simple or a two-thirds majority, depending on the matters concerned.

The Judicial and Executive Powers

The distribution of judicial and executive powers is also of great significance for the working of a federal state. The executive is the subject of part three of the 1952 Constitution. The Chief Executive or Prime Minister is assisted by executive secretaries who exercise the function of ministers. Apparently the terms 'Prime Minister' and 'Minister' were avoided, so as not to give the impression of a sovereign state. The Chief Executive is elected by parliament (Art. 68). He holds the power to name the executive secretaries, and does not require the parliament's consent for this. The vow taken by the Chief Executive is very interesting. According to Art. 72 it takes the following form:

'I undertake before Almighty God (or an invocation conforming to the faith and the customary practice of the Chief Executive) to respect the Federation under the sovereignty of the Imperial Crown, loyally to serve Eritrea, to defend its Constitution and its law, to seek the welfare of the Eritrean people in the unity of its inhabitants bound together by ties of brotherhood, whatever their race, religion or language, and to seek no personal advantage from office.'

Both the Chief Executive and the secretaries take their vow before the Emperor's representative. The parliamentary system is also of interest, but it concerns rather the relationship between the Chief Executive and the Assembly, rather than the federal or 'vertical' distribution of powers. We will therefore limit our account to a few observations. In the rules concerning the Chief Executive and his secretaries the obligation to respect the sovereignty of the Imperial Crown is expressed. Respect for the sovereignty of the Imperial dynasty and loyalty to Eritrea are thus juxtaposed, but the sovereignty of Eritrea is never mentioned. This, however, seems to me a rather academic question. Art. 77 is important for the Parliament, because it establishes the Chief Executive's right to enact orders, i.e. regulations, without the parliament's consent during those times that it is not in session. These orders later have to be presented to the Parliament for acceptance. For the administration, rules are contained in Art. 88 ff, which are too general and insufficiently detailed. Besides the Chief Executive and the Parliament, there is an Advisory Council, a sort of economic and social council. Its functions are described in Art. 84 and consist mainly in development planning, budget projection, and the drafting of statutes.

According to Art. 85, the Supreme Court wields the judicial power, together with such courts as are established in Eritrea by law. The article speaks of the application of the different legal systems which are in effect in Eritrea. The Constitution does not clarify whether Ethiopian federal law is also applied by these courts, or whether there are special federal courts. Each judge vows to be a loyal guardian of the law and that he will be impartial in his office. The independence of the judiciary is guaranteed by Art. 86, the

16

nomination of judges is regulated in Art. 87. The Chief Executive nominates judges according to a recommendation by the President of Parliament on the basis of a commission report. Both the judges and the Chief Executive are subject to the Supreme Court's jurisdiction. The Supreme Court's composition is laid down in Art. 89 and its responsibilities in Art. 90.

The Supreme Court is the highest court of appeals, both for questions of fact and of the law. It decides whether statutes and regulations are constitutional. Like the Federal Constitutional Court in the Federal Republic of Germany, it is responsible for submissions by judges (Art. 90 Sec. 3), conflicts between the Eritrean government and other constitutional bodies (Art. 90 Sec. 4), and finally for the impeachment of the Chief Executive.

The Division of Budgetary Resources

Art. 6 provides that Eritrea is to share expenditure on federal responsibilities and services justly and equitably with the Ethiopian Federation. To this end, the Ethiopian Federal Government delegates to Eritrea the power to raise taxes independently, which have to serve the common good of the Federation. This also applies to income from import and export dues. As a recompense for this contribution towards expenses, Eritrea is granted the important right of proportional representation in the Federal Executive and in Federal Courts, according to its relative population (Art. 7).

Summary

In principle, the Federal Constitution of 1952 is so structured that it could serve as the basis of a new federal order between Ethiopia and Eritrea. Other parts of Ethiopia might be given the same or another federal status, precluding a hegemonial federalism.

Some elements which were left open in 1952 to statutes- such as finances and courts- would have to be included in a new federal constitution. An additional analysis of the constitutional reality between 1952 and 1962 would make clear whether other sensitive areas require regulation in the constitution itself.

Ethiopia's historical development shows that hierarchical (vertical) and egalitarian (horizontal) structures have evolved simultaneously or successively, and these should be taken into account. The combination of both elements, which was already apparent in Ethiopia's medieval constitution and which is also expressed in the duality of Church and State, was again attempted in the 1952 Federal Constitution of Ethiopia and Eritrea.

The different degrees of modern state organisation and decentralisation - from regional autonomy to confederal or federal constitutions - offer myriad possibilities to build on historic, vertical and horizontal, traditional

17

structures. The question as to whether the head of state should be monarchical or neo-presidential, is hardly of essential importance. History provides examples of federal monarchies. Similarly a republican presidential office could take the place of the constitutional monarchy provided for under the 1952 system without making a substantial change to the federal structure.

The 1952 model could be re-applied so as to encompass only Ethiopia and Eritrea or it could be adjusted to include other areas in the federation. Of course, a federation between Eritrea and Ethiopia does not have to offer the same federal status to other peoples. A decentralised connection or regional autonomy is possible as well. But it should be noted that a federal system is preferable to a confederation. The model of 1952 ought to be improved in this respect: a second house should represent the federal states, both in legislation and administration.

In conclusion the 1952 model can be said to have accommodated the concrete historic situation, the Ethiopian-Eritrean tradition, as well as modern requirements.

---

1   H Scholler 'Herrschaft und Reich in KAthiopien - Politische Anthropologie und Verfassungsrecht' in: *Afrikastudien I, Eike Haberland zum 65, Geburtstag,* Paideuma, Mitteilungen zur Kulturkunde, Vol. 35, Wiesbaden 1989, 247.

B   Remarks on Eritrea and a Possible Framework for Peace

TESFATSION MEDHANIE

The basic aim of this chapter is to explore the idea of 'federation' as a framework for solving the Ethio-Eritrean problem. Several related issues are touched upon or briefly examined. These include the nature, the problems, and the politics of the 1952-1962 'federation'; the divisions and the issues in the Eritrean movement; the urgency for a comprehensive peace negotiations; multi-party democracy and constitutionalism; and generally the conditions for a viable federation between Ethiopia and Eritrea today. Even though the Eritrean referendum of 1993 produced an overwhelming vote for full independence, the issue of federation still remains relevant in the longer term.

The Federation: 1952-1962

One of the basic factors which precipitated or galvanised the Eritrean armed movement was the dissolution of the 'federation' in 1962. This is now, common knowledge among Eritreans, Ethiopians, and followers of the Ethio-Eritrean events. What is less known - but perhaps more important to understand and rellect on - is the essence and context of the so called 'federation' and the inevitability of its dissolution.

The 'federation' which came into effect in 1952 was sponsored by the United Nations. Juridically, it had its genesis in UN General Assembly Resolution 390A (V) - a Resolution based on a 'compromise formula' designed and put forward by the USA. The Resolution characterized Eritrea as an 'autonomous unit federated with Ethiopia under the sovereignty of the Ethiopian crown'. It did not accord to Eritrea the status of a state in a federal union with Ethiopia. Eritrea was (in the Resolution) only an autonomous region, albeit with its own

Constitution, its own Parliament, Executive and Judiciary. The UN Resolution did not provide for a 'federal' government - i.e. a government separate from and in addition to those of Ethiopia and Eritrea. It included a big section commonly known as the 'Federal Act', but did not provide for the establishment of additional governmental bodies or institutions to implement and defend it. The Resolution had provided for a 'Federal Council' - an institution which was a faint approximation to a federal body. This body - according to the Resolution - was to comprise Ethiopian and Eritrean representatives in equal numbers and advise the Emperor on matters of the 'federation'. The Council was simply ignored and practically done away with before it could even start functioning.

The UN Commissioner, Dr. Anze Matienzo, who led the UN task force that instituted the basic structures of the 'federation', adhered to the clauses of the Resolution. He gave all the 'federal' powers to the Ethiopian government - i.e. the Ethiopian government was the 'federal' government at the same time. The Ethiopian emperor was the sovereign or the Head of State in the 'federation'; the Ethiopian courts were the 'federal courts'; and the Ethiopian Ministries were the Ministries of the 'federal' government.

Furthermore, the UN Resolution had not clearly stipulated (and certainly no mechanisms were established or provided) for the UN to get involved in case Eritrea's autonomous status was violated by Ethiopia, by the 'federal' government. (It should be noted however that, in spite of this, some legal experts had opined that the UN could intervene in case the 'federation' was violated.) The whole arrangement was such that the fate of the 'federation' was in the hands of the Ethiopian government. Eritrea's status of 'autonomous unit' was quite vulnerable. It was easy for Haile Sellassie's government to interfere in Eritrean affairs and dismantle the 'federation'.

To many observers, particularly to those who had understood the nature of the Ethiopian state or government, it was clear that Ethiopia would be 'tempted' - though 'ill-advised' - to do away with Eritrea's autonomy.

What was in the nature of the Ethiopian regime which threatened the fate of Eritrea's autonomy or the fate of the 'federation'? The answer to this question readily appears from a mere contrast of the Eritrean Constitution and the Ethiopian Constitution at that time.

The Constitution of autonomous Eritrea was one modelled on those of Western democracies. It provided for three branches of government based on the rule of law. It stipulated fundamental freedoms including those of expression, conscience, and association. It provided for a multi-party system of government since one of the fundamental rights was that of association, be it in the form of trade unions or political parties.

Ethiopia then had a feudal-monarchical system of government ideologically sustained by some notion of divine right of kings. It was also avowedly 'imperial'. Haile Sellassie ruled as an absolute monarch and as head of an empire every part of which he sought to effectively subordinate to himself. The Ethiopian Constitution of 1931 provided for no political rights similar to those guaranteed in the Eritrean Constitution and in those of liberal democracies generally. (The 1955 Constitution included provisions on some aspects of liberal democracy; but even these were too circumscribed to be of considerable significance.)

As a feudal-imperial monarchy the government had a notion of territorial integrity which was incongruent with federal or other structures of decentralization. Its obsession with control and security, as well as its approaches to administration were such that it could not feel comfortable with any arrangement other than that which ensured the unitary character of the state. Hence, even Eritrea's status of mere regional autonomy was unpalatable to Haile Sellassie's regime.

As an absolute monarchist government Haile Sellassie's was naturally incapable of effectively accommodating a multi-party system of government, rule of law, and other essential features of liberal democracy in any part of the empire even if the empire was called 'federation'. It could only have been averse to the democratic institutions in the Constitution of autonomous Eritrea. It could only have felt threatened by them. As anticipated by observers the Ethiopian government openly interfered in Eritrea's internal affairs. It took successive steps to erode Eritrea's autonomy. And finally in 1962 it saw to it that the 'federation' was dissolved. Eritrea was made the 14th province of the Ethiopian Empire.

The USA and other Western powers who initiated and lobbied for the UN Resolution on Eritrea were aware of the nature and interests of Haile Sellassie's regime. They knew the 'federation' was going to be dissolved. Not only had they known, but they had accepted it. Not only had they accepted it, but it was with the 'federation's' eventual dissolution in mind that they proposed and lobbied for the 'federal' resolution. And this brings us to the politics of the Ethio-Eritrean 'federation'.

Internal and External Politics

Eritrea was the scene of divisions and internal conflicts. The divisions and conflicts reflected the history as well as the pre-national (pre-bourgeois) character of the Eritrean polity which is multi-ethnic and biconfessional. The divisions were at least accentuated by the policy of the British who administered Eritrea since 1941, the activities of the Italian government, and those of the agents and collaborators of the Ethiopian government.

The complexity of the divisions was manifested in the proliferation of political parties with diverse demands concerning the destiny of Eritrea. Many Eritreans demanded unity with Ethiopia; others immediate independence; others trusteeship (under the Italians or the British); others in effect demanded partition - or at least a different status for the western province.

The question of Eritrea could not have been resolved by giving effect to the demand of only one or some of the parties. Neither unity with Ethiopia nor Eritrean independence could have ensured peace and political stability in the country. The internal situation in Eritrea thus called for a compromise or for an appearance of a compromise.

Externally or internationally, too, the views on the destiny of Eritrea were diverse. It should be recalled that the period was the beginning of the Cold War with the USA emerging as the leader of the Western camp and wielding tremendous influence at the UN General Assembly. The USA was expanding its spheres of influence. Among other things, it was installing military bases - barely disguised as naval facilities and communication centres - in various parts of the world. The USA had appreciated the strategic location and the usefulness of Eritrea for purposes of communication.

The USA had established most friendly relations with Haile Sellassie's Ethiopia. It should be added here that Haile Sellassie's government on its part had been most eager to establish and strengthen relations with the USA.

Given the political situation in Eritrea the most certain way for the USA to gain control of Eritrea's strategic location was to bring about the annexation of Eritrea to Ethiopia.

At that time the international situation made total annexation of Eritrea to Ethiopia very difficult. The USSR, the former people's democracies in Eastern Europe, and some Afro-Arab states were aware of and opposed to USA strategy. They contended that only a separate existence - i.e. independence - could guarantee the sovereignty and progress of Eritrea. At the same time however, they were sympathetic to Ethiopia's needs for an access to the sea.

(Among the Western powers themselves there were differences of views concerning the disposal of Eritrea. The differences, which emanated from competing interests between these powers were nevertheless secondary to the then rising east/west rivalry.)

Thus on the international level too, there was a need for a compromise and for an appearance of a compromise. The Western powers reached an agreement under the auspices of the USA. The agreement was embodied in the 'compromise formula' (as they called it) which became UN Resolution 390 A (V) - the Resolution that 'federated' Eritrea with Ethiopia.

The designation of the Resolution as 'federal' was in line with the claim that it incorporated a compromise formula. The Resolution was presented as a solution that met the demands of both the pro-independence parties and the unionists half way - i.e. 'federation' was half way between separate existence (independence) and union.

But was the Resolution really such a compromise? As already mentioned the arrangement embodied in the Resolution was not 'federal' but only one which accorded to Eritrea the status of regional autonomy. The word 'federation' or 'federal' was a camouflage. It was used in order to falsely impress the pro-independence Eritrean parties that their demands were not ignored but given as much weight as those of the unionists. It was also meant to placate world opinion especially in the socialist and in some sections of the Arab-Asiatic world.

Haile Sellassie's government had demanded the full incorporation of Eritrea and nothing less. But it finally accepted the 'compromise formula'. And according to a researcher, it accepted the 'compromise' formula because of an understanding with some USA advisors. The Ethiopian government was warned that there was no way of passing a resolution on full merger, and that in order to get the necessary support at the UN there had to be a compromise in the form of a 'federal' resolution. However, once the 'federation' came into effect, Ethiopia could gradually take measures towards full incorporation.The Ethio-Eritrean 'federation' was thus structured in such a way that its erosion and final dissolution were not difficult for the Ethiopian government to realise. The 'federation' failed because it was designed to fail. At present we need an authentic federal framework to resolve the Eritrean problem. We need to design a framework that will succeed.

Before taking up the discussion on the viability of the federal framework in the case of Eritrea today a mention of the basic factor that precipitated the armed movement is in order. Eritrea had suffered political, economic, and cultural oppression under Haile Sellassie's government. This oppression gave rise to protests including some to the United Nations. The protests were in vain. As a step of last resort armed struggle for the independence of Eritrea was launched in 1961.

The new government which came to power in 1974 mishandled the Eritrean issue particularly in the early period. For several years it adhered to a militarist policy and it is only recently that it expressed readiness for negotiations without preconditions.

On the other hand external forces in collaboration with internal enemies of the regime did a lot to worsen the war situation. The government of Mengistu Haile Mariam had chosen and adhered to the socialist road. It had become an ally of the USSR. As such it had been targeted for subversion by anti-socialist forces in the West and the Middle East. These forces provided covert and indirect support to various movements, including some organisations in Eritrea who were willing to collaborate in undermining Soviet influence and Ethiopia's socialist-oriented government. Through such support they fanned the war in Eritrea.

Now, after almost 30 years of war, the situation in Eritrea is crying for peace. And a possible framework for peaceful and stable relations between Eritrea and Ethiopia is, in my opinion, federation. Federation - a genuine federation as I will point out soon - is a realistic solution. A genuine federation has the best chance of being satisfactory to both parties since in the circumstances it is a reasonable compromise solution. It can meet the interests of both peoples. On the one hand Eritrea will have a broad autonomy and equal status to the whole of Ethiopia (if Ethiopia remains a unitary state). On the other hand, Ethiopia and Eritrea would be one entity in terms of political geography, and in that sense the present territorial integrity of Ethiopia would be retained. Economically, too, federation would be gainful for both Eritrea and Ethiopia. As one economic entity they would be more productive and develop faster than they would separately. (It is quite possible that Ethiopia itself would comprise of several 'states' that are federated. In such a case Eritrea would be another state federated with the rest). If it is to become a viable solution the federation to be established should negate the USA sponsored sham 'federation' in every major respect:

(a) The federal solution should be designed considering the history of the problem and in the light of Eritrea's and Ethiopia's needs for peace, political stability, and socio-economic development. The strategic or any other kind of interest of any external power should not dominate, much less determine, the design of the federation.

(b) The establishment of the federal framework should be prefaced by Ethiopia's acknowledgment of the oppression Eritrea suffered and recognition of Eritrea's right to secede. Such acknowledgment and recognition are important as indications of or testimonies to the voluntary character of the federal union.

23

(c) The solution should have the backing of the United Nations. Everything should be done to provide the establishment of the federation with the support of the international community and the authority of international law. This is necessary as a guarantee against violation and dissolution of the federation.

(d) The structure of the Ethio-Eritrean union will have to be strictly federal. There will have to be three governments with their respective constitutions: Eritrean, Ethiopian, and the Federal government with an overall authority. (If Ethiopia itself is to consist of several federated units there would be additional state governments.)

(e) The federal constitution should embody the basic principles of democracy and safeguard civil, political, economic and cultural rights in line with international instruments like the UN Convention on Civil and Political Rights. All these fundamental rights must be entrenched in the Constitution of the Federal Union and in those of the constituent units. No one shall have the power to abrogate them except perhaps in cases of genuine national emergency duly declared in accordance with the Constitution. The Constitution should uphold multi-party democracy and the rule of law - guaranteed by the existence of an independent judiciary which interprets and protects the supremacy of the Constitution.

(f) The Constitution of the Federal Union must be the supreme law of the land. The Constitutions of Eritrea and Ethiopia (and those of such other constituent units that may exist) must be consistent with it. The Constitutions of the constituent states may differ from each other in non-basic ways in order to address particular/local situations and needs.

(g) The federation should be as integrated as possible. It should be one which does not hamper the movement of and interaction between the peoples of the constituent states. It should be easy for any citizen to acquire residence anywhere in the federation. This would facilitate the free movement of goods; it would enable the exchange or sharing of technical and other skills and expertise between the constituent states.

(h) Several features of the federal union may be replicated at the state level. For example, there could be an Eritrean flag in addition to the Federal one; working language or languages (in addition to that or those of the federation) in Eritrea (and in each of the other constituent states that may exist). The languages should be among those spoken in the respective state as are, for example, Tigrinya and Tigre in Eritrea.

(i) The composition of the federal defence force (whose size should be the minimum necessary) should reflect balanced representation of the constituent states. This will have to be carefully worked out. Police activity within the states should be a state and not a federal matter.

(j) The composition of the legislatures should be based on proportional representation (PR). There are several variants of PR. One of the variants, which I personally think is viable in Eritrea and Ethiopia, is the List System (which for example is what they have in Namibia). Under this system people vote for two or more political parties contesting for seats in the Parliament. Each party issues a list of names of candidates for seats. Each party is given a number of seats and thus represented in the legislature in proportion to the votes it received.

Obviously such a federation cannot be established right away. At the stage of negotiations as well as at that of designing the structure of the federation caution should be exercised to ensure that things are done in the interest of peace and democracy. Caution is all the more necessary given the nature of the situation in the Eritrean movement and the danger it poses to democracy.

The Eritrean Movement Today

It is necessary to examine briefly the politics and generally the situation of the Eritrean movement today. Such an examination would help one to identify better the requisite conditions for democracy in Eritrea and Ethiopia and for a viable federation between them.

There are still serious divisions in the Eritrean movement. There are several organizations. The Eritrean People's Liberation Front (EPLF) is militarily the strongest, but politically it is not necessarily the most popular in the country. The other organisations - militarily much weaker - could very well have a bigger number of followers particularly if they effectively co-ordinate or join hands under some sort of umbrella organisation.

It is important to bear in mind what kind of movement the EPLF is. As an organisation the EPLF is quite efficient. This quality, together with other factors, has made it militarily effective. However, this organisation is anti-democratic. Throughout the years it has attacked and suppressed democratic-minded intellectuals and other patriots inside and outside the organisation.

Ever since its emergence, and especially since the mid-seventies, the EPLF played sectarian and divisive roles in the Eritrean movement. It is still playing the same roles. It has refused to recognise the existence of - much less to unite with - the Eritrean Liberation Front (ELF- RC) and other organisations. The EPLF, by itself, cannot bring about democracy or ensure inter-ethnic and interconfessional peace in Eritrea.

It should be realised that the EPLF came to dominate the armed movement, to a large extent because of the support it got from the forces of anti-socialism in the West, the Middle East, and the Horn of Africa. These forces had targeted the then 'pro-Soviet', socialist-oriented government in Addis Ababa. They needed to strengthen movements in Eritrea and Ethiopia that were 'anti-Derg', and anti-Soviet. It did not matter that the rhetoric of some of these movements was Marxist. So long as they were 'anti-Soviet' they were deemed worth supporting. In Eritrea such a movement was the EPLF, and in Ethiopia the Tigrai People's Liberation Front (TPLF).

The other major organisation in Eritrea - the ELF (RC) - was on the other hand condemned by the forces of anti-socialism as a 'pro-Soviet' movement inclined towards negotiations and peace with Addis Ababa. The EPLF and TPLF, supported in subtle ways by the Sudan, Iraq, Somalia, and other nearby states attacked the ELF. In 1980-81 they waged war on the ELF. In that war which continued for over a year Nimeiri's Sudan played some roles which contributed to the military defeat and political problems of the ELF (RC).

The purpose behind supporting the EPLF and TPLF was either to bring about the downfall of the government in Addis Ababa or to pressure the government to such an extent that it would be forced to abandon the socialist road.

In light of the above the following should be emphasised in respect of the negotiations:

(1) The negotiations should begin as early as possible. A viable federal framework that may be agreed upon now can, and should, continue after the present government is succeeded by another.

(2) The negotiations should be as inclusive as is practicable. They should not be with the EPLF alone. All the major Eritrean organisations should equally participate. (The main shortcoming in the effort of the Carter Centre regarding peace talks on Eritrea has been that only the EPLF - to the exclusion of the other Eritrean organisations - was represented on the Eritrean side).

On this issue some EPLF supporters are still advocating ideas that are rather uncalled for. Such a supporter is Lionel Cliffe. Cliffe does not seem to recognise that Eritrean organisations other than the EPLF are worth negotiating with. In October 1989 he wrote describing the 'ELF factions' as having only 'some presence in exile circles'. He asserted: 'In terms of negotiations for peace they are irrelevant' (*Third World Quarterly*, Oct. 1989, p. 139). However the ELF groups did have some military presence inside Eritrea. But, more importantly, they have strong social bases and considerable political followers both inside and outside Eritrea. They are as relevant to the peace process in Eritrea as the EPLF is. Exclusion of these organisations - i.e a separate deal or separate negotiations with the EPLF- only guarantees the perpetuation of internal conflict and instability in Eritrea.

Incidentally, as a federated unit, how is Eritrea to be administered? Or more precisely, how is the leadership of Eritrea to be constituted? A realistic view on this question must proceed from a recognition of one unfortunate reality in the Eritrean movement, which is that there can be no unity based on equality between the EPLF and other Eritrean organisations. For many years the EPLF has refused to unite with the others. At the moment it does not even recognise their existence.

This is a very serious problem. But there is a solution, and this solution is the system of Proportional Representation which was applied in Namibia. Let the various parties or organisations contest in free and fair elections supervised by third parties. That way the people decide to what extent they trust and mandate each of them: the ELF, the EPLF, ELF-RC, ELF-PLF etc.. All these parties (and other parties that may be established) will be represented in the Eritrean state assembly in proportion to the votes they receive in the elections.

In these remarks an attempt has been made to underline the importance of political democracy as a vital component of any 'federal' system. In our case it is only too obvious that the idea of a federal framework should include a genuine commitment to democracy throughout the 'federation', including Eritrea.

3 Ethnicity and the National Question in Ethiopia

CHRISTOPHER CLAPHAM

The twentieth century rallying cry of national self-determination which was taken up as a mechanism for dismembering the Austro-Hungarian empire at the start of the century, and is being seized on once again as a mechanism for dismembering the Soviet one at the end of it - raises intense and familiar problems in defining the 'nation', and characterising the common identity of those who constitute it. This task has been complicated in many parts of the world, Ethiopia included, by the introduction and application of ideologies of national self-determination initially articulated in a very different (and usually European) setting, and their adoption as instruments of domestic political debate. The analysis by the Tigray People's Liberation Front (TPLF) in 1986 of its differences with the Eritrean People's Liberation Front (EPLF) in terms of the correct interpretation of Stalin's view of the national question provides only one of the more bizarre examples[1]. Since the nature of nationality or ethnicity in Ethiopia is thus a contested element in conflicts within the country, and since identities themselves have been reshaped - and continue to be reshaped - in the course of the traumatic experiences that the people of the region have endured. Any academic examination of the nature and role of ethnicity in Ethiopia is peculiarly difficult. Some such examination is nonetheless needed as a background to the current conflicts, and the prospects for their solution.

27

The Bases and Limitations of Central Ethiopian Nationalism

Ethiopia is distinctive in modern Africa as the recognisable successor to an ancient indigenous African state, and the starting point for any analysis must, therefore, be the historic Ethiopian state and the social bases on which it rested. People from other groups have increasingly and justifiably protested at the monopolisation of Ethiopian 'history' by the Amharic and Tigrinya speaking peoples, sometimes conveniently lumped together as Abyssinians, who have formed the core of that state. A conscious attempt is being made to rectify the marginalisation of the historical experience of other indigenous peoples through a revisionist historiography of the region[2]. However, even the revisionists have not denied - and indeed they have generally emphasised - the military and political dominance of the central state, which has thus played the key role in defining the nature and impact of ethnicity in the country as a whole.

Though 'nationalism' is a social construct which can scarcely be applied to Ethiopia before the mid-twentieth century, Abyssinian society had a cultural basis which both aided the maintenance of a multi-ethnic political system over a considerable length of time, and provided some foundation for the creation of a modern Ethiopian nationalism. Central to this was the fact that Abyssinian society was not 'tribal', in the technical but very important sense that it was not based on a mythology of descent. The term 'tribe' has of course been much used and abused in the discussion of African ethnicity, with the understandable result that many scholars have wished to dispense with it altogether. The idea that all the people in a given group are related by blood to one another, characteristically through descent from a mythological common ancestor in either the male or the female line, has nonetheless had a powerful effect on the character of ethnicity in many African societies, and has introduced a rigidity into social relationships that has profoundly influenced the nature of African politics. To take one familiar example from the Horn, the Somali people not only share a myth of descent in the male line from a common ancestor - Somal - which defines them as Somali: the myth of descent from Somal's sons and grandsons defines the further clan groupings - Darod, Dir, Isaq - and the individual clans that form the basis for political allegiance and segmentation within Somali society[3]. Other peoples of the Horn, such as the Oromo and Gurage, have shared similar mythologies of descent, though in each case these have been modified as a result of social change and contact with Abyssinian society.

A society that does *not* share a genealogical basis for its identity is thus anomalous. In Abyssinian society, descent was recognised on something approaching equal terms through both male and female lines. Land rights - the critical productive resource in an economy which, uniquely in sub-Saharan Africa, was based on plough agriculture - could be inherited through either mother or father. Rights in animals, and notably the oxen which were needed to pull the plough, were likewise vested in both men and women. The social significance of this simple fact is enormous: an individual has only one father, one father's father, and one father's father's father but two parents, four grandparents, and eight great-grandparents. This gives one myriad lines of descent, enabling one to maximise one's access to resources by mobilising whichever line is likely to prove most beneficial. Politically, it has had the effect of systematically blurring descent, and enabling individuals to associate themselves with the ancestry of their most important forebears, or indeed with peoples from whom they were not descended at all. To take one striking example: Emperor Haile Selassie's father's father was Oromo; his father's mother was Amhara: his mother's father was Oromo; and his mother's mother was Gurage. In a patrilineal society he would have been classed as Oromo, in a matrilineal one as Gurage; but to all intents and purposes he was Amhara, and it was his descent from his father's mother, a member of the Shoan royal house, that provided the genealogical basis for his claim to the Imperial throne.

This fluidity has permitted a level of political assimilation which has been evident at least since the mid-eighteenth century, when Oromo leaders started to gain positions of prominence in the Ethiopian central government. It has been much more marked among the Amhara than among the Tigreans, partly perhaps because of internal reasons (such as the communal system of Tigrean land tenure), but largely because of political geography. The Tigrean lands, at the northern end of the Abyssinian plateau, were bordered on three sides by Moslem peoples who were difficult to assimilate, and had very limited opportunities for expansion; since they were also poor and overpopulated, Tigreans have tended to emigrate to other areas of Ethiopia. The Amhara peoples to the south, on the other hand, were ideally placed to expand their control into what is now southern and western Ethiopia - a process involving conquest, land alienation and a great deal of exploitation, but also offering at least some opportunity for assimilating conquered peoples into an expanded Ethiopian state. The Shoan region around Addis Ababa, for example, is overwhelmingly Oromo in ethnic composition, and a very high proportion of those who pass for Shoan Amharas are partly or wholly of Oromo descent. But anyone with an Amharic name who speaks Amharic and adheres to Orthodox Christianity, to all intents and purposes *is* Amhara, and is fully accepted as such by other Amharas. No charter of genealogical acceptability, real or mythical, is required. Whereas in most of Africa, any prominent politician is instantlly identifiable in terms of his ancestry, including not only his tribe but usually the clan or section within it, this is not the case in Ethiopia. There is, for example, no convincing and generally acknowledged account of the parentage of Mengistu Haile-Mariam. Most reports place his paternal ancestry broadly in the area of southern Ethiopia, conquered in the late nineteenth century, where northern Sidamo, southern Shoa and eastern Kaffa regions adjoin one another, and it is usually suggested that his father was a Wollayta. It is likewise widely suggested that he is related by blood to the family of a Shoan nobleman in whose household he was reared, either through his mother or as the illegitimate son of the nobleman himself. But this is no more than speculation, and his genealogical obscurity made no difference to his ability to rule Ethiopia for fourteen years. The origins of many leading members of his government were equally unknown.

The Ethiopian system of personal nomenclature is also worth noting.

An Ethopian's name normally consists of his own personal name, followed by his father's personal name. Mengistu Haile-Mariam is Mengistu, the son of Haile-Mariam. His father's name was Haile-Mariam Lencho; his children bear their own first name. followed by Mengistu as a patronymic. It is a system with a very short memory, in which an individual's origins are unidentifiable beyond his father's generation. It is quite common to find people - like Haile-Selassie's finance minister Yilma Deressa, or Derg member Debele Dinsa - with an Amharic personal name and an Oromo patronymic; but as a conventional process of giving children Amharic names continues, many non-Amharas (like Mengistu himself) become ethnically unidentifiable.

Up to a point, a generalised Amharic identity has thus become the basis for an inclusive Ethiopian nationalism that can no longer be associated solely with a single ethnic group or nationality. The Amharic language, for example, has become widely dispersed throughout Ethiopia, and is the only country-wide medium of communication. This identity has been most readily accepted by smaller groups in Southern Ethiopia, who have become associated with the Ethiopian state and have no evident future outside it. Many of these peoples, though incorporated into Ethiopia only in the later nineteenth century, have no record of supporting insurgent or separatist movements, and - at least up to the present - appear to see no clash between their own local identities and membership of a larger national political unit. Gurages and Kambattas in southern Shoa, Kaffas and Kulo Kontas in Kaffa, Sidamas and Wollaytas in Sidamo are all examples. At the same time, it is all too evident that in a state so riven by conflict as Ethiopia, any picture of a country going through a process of 'nation-building' through the simple extension of an Amharic identity is very seriously short of the mark. The process of homogenisation which has a certainly been taking place in Ethiopia over the last half-century and more has at the same time been accompanied by - and has contributed to - a corresponding process of ethnic conflict and differentiation.

Before looking at the way in which ethnicity has progressively become politicised in Ethiopia, however, it is essential to point out that many of the current and recent conflicts have not in any meaningful sense been ethnic at all, or have included ethnicity only as one element among others. Were it not that it has become almost automatic to ascribe any conflict (especially but not only in Africa) to ethnicity, it would scarcely be necessary to point out that people fight about many other things as well. Independently of any question of ethnicity, the Mengistu regime was one which many Ethiopians felt driven to oppose, and given that it allowed no opportunity for legitimate dissent, those who opposed it openly and within the country had no option but to do so through insurgent warfare in those parts of the country - notably the northern highlands - where this was a viable strategy. Indeed, the EPRDF insurgency which eventually overthrew the regime was drawn from the heartland of the Ethiopian state, in Tigray, Gonder and Wollo regions, and could only very partially be regarded as an ethnic or 'nationality' movement. Nonetheless, ethnicity cannot be entirely ignored, and three broad (and obviously linked) elements can be distinguished that have helped to contribute to it. These are the pattern of state formation, the pattern of social and economic change and the effects of the revolution of 1974.

Ethnicity and the Pattern of State Formation

The pattern of state formation is the reverse side of precisely the same process that gave the Amharic language, culture and identity a quasi-national status. Regardless of the relative openness of the Amharic culture to the assimilation of other peoples, the definition of this culture as a national and implicitly superior one simultaneously defined the lesser status of every other - a definition reinforced by the imposition of central control and a substantial level of physical brutality and economic exploitation.

The core of the modern Ethiopian central state lies in the region of Shoa, which was ideally placed to combine the advantages of political dominance with those of economic developmont. Until the nineteenth century Shoa was a peripheral region in the old Ethiopian empire. Its Amhara populations were at times virtually cut off by Oromo incursions from the then central regions of Gonder, Tigray and Wollo. But its geographical location, with a succession of dynamic leaders from King Sahle-Selassie (1813-1847) onwards, enabled it to spearhead the expansion that within a century had made it the geographical centre of a vastly greater territory. The new permanent capital of Addis Ababa was placed by Emperor Menilek (1889-1913) in the Oromo lands which for the previous three centuries had been on the borders of Ethiopia. The new communications network was centred there, as were the government, the educational system, and all the apparatus of the modern state. A new class of officials, overwhelmingly Shoan, grew up around the court of a Shoan emperor. It would certainly be an exaggeration to regard modern Ethiopia as simply a Shoan state, or to see Ethiopian nationalism as just a rationale for Shoan domination. But the core position of Shoa, and its association with the imposition of the modern state and the statist ideology that helped to sustain it, were progressively reinforced during the century after Menilek's accession. This aroused resentment not only from the newly incorporated peoples, but from those of historic Ethiopia as well.

Some peoples, notably the pastoralists, but also the peoples of the western borderlands, have had little more than a marginal stake in the expanded Ethiopian state. The role of the largest of these, the Somalis, has effectively been governed by the tension between the attraction of a single Somali state on the one hand, and the intense divisions between different Somali clan groupings on the other; the central Ethiopian state has not so much incorporated them, as sought to manage their internal conflicts in such a way as to neutralise the threat which they presented. The Afars, up until the revolution, were governed through a mixture of indifference and indirect rule. Both Somalis and Afars were in any event Moslems, as were some but not all of the pastoral Oromo - the Boran Oromo being the major exception. Islam in itself placed a considerable, though not absolutely insuperable, barrier in the way of incorporation into a state dominated by

Orthodox Christians: the Moslem Oromo of eastern Wollo and Tigray have been associated with the state for over two centuries, and the Adere people of the city of Harar - a small and highly educated group - have also reached positions of political prominence, but these are the exception. The rapid spread of Islam in much of southern Ethiopia during the twentieth century may be seen as a process of explicit differentiation from, and rejection of, the dominant Orthodox state[4]. In other southern regions such as Welega, however, the adoption of western forms of Christianity provided educational opportunities which offered the chance to participate in national government

The experience of conquest and land alienation thus created rather different legacies in different areas of the south. In Welega and some other regions, local notables were able to reach an accommodation with the encroaching Ethiopian state which allowed them to retain office as the representatives of the central power, and in the process act as a buffer between central and local interests[5]. In others, the conquest was a much more brutal affair, and the subsequent level of land alienation was correspondingly greater. Land alienation, too, took different forms. Some areas, such as Arsi, were handed over as vast estates to leading members of Menilek's Shoan administration. Others, such as parts of Hararge, were divided into small plots among settlers known as *neftenya*. The physical endowment and indigenous agricultural systems of southern Ethiopia also made a difference. The pastoralist areas were not greatly affected until the post-1941 era, when permanent watercourses (notably in the Awash valley) were turned over to irrigated cash-crop agriculture, often managed by foreign corporations. Grain growing areas, in contrast, were readily taken over by settlers who reduced the indigenous populations to the level of serfs. Coffee-growing zones, which were generally thinly inhabited, were much sought after by central landlords from the 1940s onwards. Areas of *enset* cultivation, which sustained high population densities but were unamenable to cash-crop production, often retained a substantial degree of local economic autonomy.

These differences created varying reactions to central power, which were especially important for the most numerous of all Ethiopia's peoples, the Oromo. An ethnic map of Ethiopia reveals substantial Oromo populations in every one of its fifteen regions apart from Gonder and Eritrea. In southern Ethiopia, non-Oromo peoples (apart from the Afar and Somali) appear almost as islands within an Oromo ocean. But the process of Oromo expansion which created this effect was achieved at the cost of increasing differentiation amongst the Oromo themselves. Those of Wollo and Tigray, occupying the buffer zone between the Amhara-Tigrean highlands and the Afar of the Red Sea plains, have for centuries been virtually isolated from the populations to the south. Shoan Oromos, many of them Orthodox Christian and benefiting from their place in the dominant region of modern Ethiopia, have become more closely associated than any others with the central power: they have taken more prominent positions in central government than Amharas from the northern regions, and many of the Shoan settlers in the south were themselves Oromos, like the local populations on whom they were imposed - even though, coming from

Shoa in the army of an Ethiopian emperor, professing Orthodox Christianity, and often speaking Amharic, they were classed as Amharas by their subject peoples[6]. For these subject peoples, on the other hand, notably those in the historic centre of Ethiopian Islam in Hararge region, religion, exploitation and ethnicity combined to resist assimilation. The Oromo of the south-west were Islamised likewise, but retained elements of a separate identify derived from the historic Oromo states of the region. Welega in the west, as already noted, is the main centre of Ethiopian protestantism, expressed through the Lutheran church *Mekane Yesus*. The pastoral Boran in southern Sidamo are the only Oromo to have retained the traditional Oromo age-grade structure into the modern era. Despite attempts in recent decades to mobilise an Oromo identity, notably through the Oromo Liberation Front (OLF), this has, therefore, been greatly impeded by the diversity of the Oromo experience of incorporation into Ethiopia.

In one region, Eritrea, the pattern of late nineteenth and twentieth century state formation was reversed: whereas what is now southern Ethiopia was incorporated into an expanding Ethiopian state of which it had not previously been part, much of Eritrea comprised people and territory which had formed part of Ethiopia from the very earliest times, but were then excised from it by Italian colonialism. Eritrea is as much an ethnic mosaic as the rest of Ethiopia. The Tigrinya-speaking peoples of the central plateau provinces of Hamasen, Seray and Akale Guzay were before 1890 as 'Ethiopian' as those of northern Shoa, Wollo or Gojjam; as the most numerous and densely settled people in the territory, occupying the areas around the capital, Amhara, they acquired a central position within Eritrea that was roughly equivalent to that of the Amhara within Ethiopia as a whole. The Tigre-speaking peoples further north, though of Ethiopian ethnic and linguistic origin, had during the period of central government decline become progressively separated from the rest of Ethiopia, a process indicated by conversion to Islam. The Afar and Saho of the Red Sea plain, and the Moslem peoples of western Eritrea had at times been brought under tenuous Ethiopian control (the port of Massawa was Ethiopian until the 1550s), but were not incorporated into the structure of the state. Even though many Tigrinya-speakers retained an emotional attachment to Ethiopia, Italian colonialism helped to create a pattern of social and economic development which distanced Eritrea from the regions to the south.

Ethnicity and Social Change

From the late nineteenth century onwards, Ethiopian rulers needed to construct a 'modern' state, with access to external education, technology, and armaments. This required a source of foreign exchange, which - just as in neighbouring colonial territories - called for the creation of an export capacity in agricultural primary products. The most important of these has consistently been coffee, though other products such as hides and skins, pulses, and at times grain, have also been involved. For both social and economic-reasons this export economy - together with the increasing

33

domestic cash economy created by urbanisation and the spread of communications - was heavily concentrated in the centre and south of the country. Climatically, coffee grew at middle altitudes across the south of the country from Harar in the east to Kaffa in the west. New lines of communication, notably the railway from Djibouti to Addis Ababa and roads radiating out from the capital to the south and west, provided access to the outside world which cut out the historic route to the sea through Massawa on the Eritrean coast. Communications in the south of the country were in any case much easier than in the ravine-dissected north. Socially, the conquest of the south created a subject population who could be much more readily exploited for the market than the Amharas and Tigreans of the northern plateau, who retained traditional social hierarchies and land tenure systems which no emperor could interfere with. The Shoan generals, courtiers and settlers who were allocated lands in the south were interested in profits, and hence in cash crops, rather than in an indigenous subsistence agriculture. Exploitative this process certainly was, but it shifted the economic centre of Ethiopia away from the northern highlands towards the newly conquered south. Not only was the north progressively marginalised in the new economy; it became progressively less able to sustain even the old one. The decline of the northern subsistence economy has continued, despite considerable fluctuation, from the great famine of the late 1880s and early 1890s through to the present day.

In Eritrea, the situation was rather different. Intended as a colony for Italian settlement, it received a substantial amount of investment which helped to make Asmara a major urban centre, and led to modest industrialisation. A road network was built, along with a railway from the coast at Massawa. Though formal opportunities for Eritrean education were negligible (and quite a number of educated Eritreans found posts in the imperial government in Addis Ababa), Eritreans were drawn into a modern cash economy, and acquired some of the skills which went with it. The Eritrean economy was further boosted in the 1930s by the fascist invasion of Ethiopia. The subsequent period of neglect and decline, first under British adminstration and then under the 1952 federation with Ethiopia, gave Eritrea an experience of economic marginalisation which was intensified by the contrast with its previous level of development.

As happened throughout Africa, uneven economic change thus created many of the conditions for the growth of modern ethnicity; but in Ethiopia these changes tended to run counter to the pattern of political inclusion and exclusion derived from the historically dominant role of the northern highlanders. While both political and economic factors reinforced the central position of Shoa, the process of economic change helped to incorporate the southern regions more firmly into Ethiopia, while the historic northern regions were economically neglected - and, increasingly, politically alienated.

The Legacy of Revolution

Though both economic exploitation and political alienation helped to promote the overthrow of the imperial regime in 1974, and though the new political groups that emerged from this experience sought to resolve both of these problems, the effect of revolution was to intensify the process of ethnic and regional differentiation. Despite the intense conflicts between revolutionary groupings that culminated in the terror of 1976-78, there was a substantial level of underlying agreement about what the problems were, and how they should be rectified. The end of economic exploitation required a thoroughgoing land reform, under which the private ownership of land was abolished, and control over rural land was returned to local communities which were organised into peasants' associations. The social basis of exploitation in southern Ethiopia was thus removed by the destruction of the landlord and settler class that had maintained it. Although land reform failed to achieve its second objective of promoting agricultural development by releasing the productive energies of the peasantry, it was outstandingly successful in removing the major form of social and economic oppression in southern Ethiopia, and goes a long way to expain why most of this area remained politically quiescent for the subsequent 15 years.

The attempt to create a new social and political basis for the Ethiopian state was much less successful. The abolition of the constitutional status of Orthodox Christianity, and the formal equality of Christianity and Islam, could make little difference to a political structure in which the state was overwhelmingly in the hands of Christian highlanders. Attempts to devolve political authority by appointing regional administrators to their own regions of origin foundered in the face of conflicts in Addis Ababa, especially because most of the new regional politicians supported political movements such as Meison, which eventually fell out with the Mengistu regime. A formal recognition of the right to 'national self-determination' rapidly became meaningless, as power was monopolised by a ruthlessly centralising group of jacobins, for whom any expression of regional identity was treasonable.

It is, nonetheless, important to emphasise that the Mengistu regime was vastly more successful in managing the newly conquered regions of southern Ethiopia than the 'historic' provinces of the north. Apart from the Somali war of 1977-8, southern Ethiopia provided little effective overt opposition to the regime until late in the 1980s, when organised opposition from the Oromo Liberation Front (OLF) started to emerge. This opposition, moreover, operated in two widely separated theatres, Hararge and western Welega, which offered opportunities to operate across the frontiers from Somalia and Sudan. In Welega especially, it made use of Oromo soldiers from the central army, who had been captured by the ELF and TPLF in the north, and were then moved south through the Sudan and infiltrated into western Ethiopia. Even in Eritrea, the initial opposition to Ethiopian rule mounted by the Moslem peoples of the lowlands through the Eritrean Liberation Front (ELF) was progressively displaced from the later 1970s by the Eritrean People's Liberation Front (EPLF), which drew the greater part of its leadership and support from the Tigrinya-speaking Christian highlanders who until colonisation had formed part of the Ethiopian state.

I have sought elsewhere to explain this paradox basically in terms of the marginalisation of the northern Ethiopian economy: the collapse of the subsistence economy in the face of population pressure, land degradation and uncertain rainfall; the lack of export production to tie the region into the international economy; and the long-term decline of the cash economy introduced in Eritrea by Italian colonialism[7]. Land reform in northern Ethiopia inhibited emigration and locked the peasantry into their shrinking subsistence plots; and in an area where peasants largely controlled their own means of production, the nationalisation of land was implicitly threatening rather than liberating. The revolutionary regime's disastrous prohibition on the private hire of agricultural labour, devised as a means of preventing exploitation, not only reduced cash crop production but deprived northern peasants of seasonal economic opportunities which they had needed in order to compensate for the decline of subsistence asriculture. This economic failure was then compounded by political and military repression.

Even in southern Ethiopia, the regime was progressively losing the initial support which land reform had given it. The intensified exactions of the central government, through increased taxes on export production and the imposition of grain production quotas, reduced and probably reversed the gains made through not having to pay rent to landlords. Further impositions were made to meet the demands of warfare, notably through military conscription. The villagisation campaign, through which peasants were herded into centralised villages permitting a much higher level of government control, can only have had a profoundly depressing effect on peasant production and morale. Though villagisation, and the equally disastrous agricultural cooperativisation (or collectivisation) campaign, were reversed by Mengistu's belated policy reforms in 1990, it could only have been a matter of time before resistance grew in the south. As it was, disaffection in southern Ethiopia played little active role in overthrowing the regime, even though by early 1991 the largely southern army on which that regime depended was no longer prepared to fight for it.

The role of specifically ethnic factors in the resistance to the Mengistu regime was thus ambivalent. Even though opposition to a ruthlessly centralising and nationalist regime might well have been expected to take an ethnic form, the only explicitly ethnic movement, the OLF, was of only limited effectiveness and scarcely even reached the point at which it would have to confront the ambivalence of Oromo ethnicity. Resistance in Eritrea, once the EPLF had succeeded in driving out the ELF in the late 1970s, took a national and multi-ethnic form, in keeping with the EPLF's determination to achieve independence within the Italian colonial boundaries, and its need to overcome religious and ethnic differences within the territory. The TPLF opposition was able to draw on the specifically Tigrean element within the Abyssinian core, but presented this in the form of a demand for regional autonomy (within an expanded Tigray region) rather than secession. As the scope of the movement spread, it developed into the Ethiopian People's Revolutionary Democratic Front (EPRDF), a coalition which included Amhara and Oromo elements, as well as representatives of marginal peoples such as those of the Gambela salient. This involved a further playing down of ethnicity, even before it took control of the central government in May 1991. Even under the most favourable circumstances of widespread opposition to a centralising regime, the role of ethnicity was thus surprisingly muted.

Conclusion : The New Politics of Nationality

The overthrow of the Mengistu government in May 1991 amounted to more than the collapse of a particular regime. It effectively marked the failure of a project, dating back to Menilek's accession in 1889 of creating a 'modern' and centralised Ethiopian state around a Shoan core. This project, which provided the unifying theme of Haile-Selassie's long reign, was tested to self-destruction by a revolutionary regime which provoked a level of resistance that eventually culminated in the appearance of Tigrean guerrillas on the streets of Addis Ababa - a dramatic reversal of the process which, over the previous century, had seen central armies moving out to incorporate and subdue the periphery.

This collapse calls into question both the power of the state, and its composition: any viable structure of government must involve both a considerable degree of decentralisation, inevitably accompanied by the extension of ethnic and regional forms of political identity, and a reduction in what government at *any* level seeks to do. The attempt to create a strong and centralised state in one of the poorest countries in the world proved to be economically unsustainable as well as politically disastrous. This is, indeed, a fact that the leaders of the interim Ethiopian People's Revolutionary Democratic Front (EPRDF) administration, showing a pragmatism startlingly at variance with their previous espousal of a peculiarly doctrinaire form of Marxism, have been very quick to recognise. The creation of an effective structure of government in the wake of the collapse of centralism nonetheless arouses a complex set of issues.

One element which may in a sense be treated separately is the future of Eritrea. The EPRDF's victory in Addis Ababa was followed by the uncontested takeover by the EPLF of the whole of Eritrea; and although any declaration of independence was postponed, the EPRDF leadership made it clear that it neither could, nor would, oppose any movement to independence approved by the Eritrean people. A *de facto* independence was thus already in place. The EPLF's adherence to the principle of territorial integrity within the Italian colonial boundaries, and its belief (despite the recognition of different 'nationalities' within Eritrea) in an Eritrean nationalism which establishes the core position of the Tigrinya-speaking highlanders, nonetheless raises many of the same questions that the Mengistu regime had faced in Ethiopia. The EPLF, its self-confidence boosted by victory at the end of a long war, may, indeed, be regarded as the last adherent in the Horn of the ideology of the centralised multiethnic state. But the extent to which the EPLF has, as its adherents claim, forged a new and national Eritrean identity in the heat of a war of liberation remains to be tested in peacetime conditions. The potential clash between a statehood derived from colonial partition and indigenous ethnic identities may also be exacerbated by the fact that the Tigrinya-speakers straddle the border with the rest of Ethiopia, while the Afars cross over both into

Ethiopia and into Djibouti as well. Any mobilisation of sub-national identities within Eritrea thus carries considerable risks of cross-border tension.

The longer term future of an independent Eritrea depends on whether the EPLF is capable of transforming its extraordinary military efficiency into an effective structure of domestic government and economic management. There is no guarantee that it will be able to do so. Vietnam and Cambodia provide striking examples of states which have failed to convert military triumph into peacetime success - largely, it would seem to me, because of a mistaken assumption that the mechanisms of control that work so well in wartime can be used to meet the very different demands of civil life. The EPLF may well be wiser; but it inherits a war-torn territory with a poor resource base, the political and economic viability of which remains open to question.

In the remainder of Ethiopia, the restraints on the mobilisation of ethnic identities imposed by a succession of centralising regimes have, for the moment at least, been lifted; and since Ethiopia has never passed through the period of open politicisation and party formation that the waning of colonialism brought to other parts of Africa, the consequences are both unpredictable and potentially disruptive. Unlike the period of African nationalist mobilisation in the 1950s and early 1960s, there is none of the unifying impetus provided by the common struggle against colonialism. And, whereas in the earlier period there were very strong international constraints, both within Africa and in the global system as a whole, against the fragmentation of existing territorial units, these have been replaced by a remarkable international willingness - triggered by events in the Soviet Union - to accept and even encourage separatist demands for the formation of new states. Eritrean independence provides, as Ethiopian rulers have long feared, a tempting precedent for any other region or ethnic constituency that wishes to go its own way.

Yet the political geography of Ethiopia offers few ready-made opportunities for further fragmentation. The peoples on the very periphery of the Ethiopian state, with fewest links to the central power structure, are currently inhibited from secession by conditions beyond the frontier. The Afar, whose territory forms a natural ethnic and ecological unit, are held back by the clash between an Afar nationalism and the identity and integrity of Eritrea. A Somali state which has collapsed into chaos and bloodshed can offer little attraction to the Somalis of the Ogaden. For the Sudanic peoples of south-west Ethiopia, there can likewise be little allure in exchanging an Ethiopian central government for a Sudanese one. The flow of refugees in both south-east and south-west Ethiopia, always a sensitive reflection of conditions on either side of the border, currently shows far more people coming into Ethiopia than leaving it.

The remaining peoples of southern Ethiopia may crudely be divided into Oromo and non-Oromo. For the latter, who notably include the numerous and densely settled peoples of the *enset* culture, there is much to be said for a measure of local autonomy, but little plausible basis for independence. They have as yet generated no viable separatist movements, and if the fragmentation of Ethiopia came to the top of the political agenda, there would be much to be said for incorporation into a larger unit, than for subordination to an inevitably Oromo-dominated government in a new, artificial and uncertain southern Ethiopian state.

This raises the issue of the Oromo, on which in essence the future of Ethiopia depends. There has for some 15 years been a movement, the OLF, which has sought to mobilise an Oromo ethnic identity, as the base on which to form an independent Oromo state. The collapse of the Mengistu government gives it a fairly free hand despite the existence of a rival movement, the Oromo People's Democratic Organisation (OPDO), formed under the aegis of the EPRDF to extend its appeal throughout the Oromo lands. And there are substantial Oromo populations, notably the Moslem Oromo of Hararge and very possibly those of Arsi and northern Bale, for whom an independent Oromo state may have a considerable attraction. The problems lie both in the geographical scatter of the Oromo-inhabited areas, and in the difficulty of creating any Oromo identity that serves anything more than the negative role of pointing up the contrast with an Ethiopian one; and even this, given the integration of many Oromo into the Ethiopian state and society, is problematical. For the Oromo moreover, as for Ethiopia as a whole, Shoa occupies a pivotal position. An Oromo state which amounted to more than a collection of barely contiguous fragments would need to include the region surrounding Addis Ababa, which would then presumably return to its original Oromo name of Finfine. It would start to look very much like a truncated Ethiopia.

There remains the legacy of Ethiopian statehood itself. It would be hard to exaggerate the horror with which many Ethiopian nationalists viewed the irruption of the EPRDF guerrillas onto the streets of Addis Ababa. Little though they liked the Mengistu regime, they had generally come to accept it as the only viable alternative to national fragmentation, with the result that once that regime collapsed, there was no available political structure or leadership through which the centralist tendency in Ethiopia could be represented. A few small demonstrations in the immediate aftermath of the EPRDF takeover indicated a determination to ensure that the centralist position was not entirely ignored. The Ethiopian People's Revolutionary Party (EPRP), who had formed a small guerrilla insurgency in western Gojiam after their expulsion from Addis Ababa in the terror of 1976-8, and who had ineffectually contested the EPRDF advance through Goiiam in early 1991, came almost by default to stand for an Ethiopian identity, in the face of the forces of fragmentation grouped into the EPRDF.

Yet, not only has Ethiopia maintained a tradition of statehood which has survived over many centuries, and surfaced even after long periods of eclipse; this tradition is built into the very machinery of government through which any future regime will have to rule. The EPRDF has dissolved the army and even the police force of the old regime, and intends to reconstruct them in accordance with its own model of democratic institutions. But given that a state is necessary - and the collapse of the state in the Somali Republic and Liberia provides the most powerful argument for its retention - many of the institutions and personnel of the old Ethiopian state are likely to remain, and to carry with them the traditions of a society in which government, order and hierarchy have long been respected. Indeed, the astonishing ease and lack of bloodshed with which the EPRDF takeover of Addis Ababa was accomplished testified not only to the absence of support for the Mengistu regime, but to an acceptance both by the EPRDF and by the surviving institutions of the old regime that order and government were essential to existence. The contrast with Monrovia and Mogadishu could scarcely be more striking. The tension within Ethiopia between the forces of centralism and those of fragmentation has not been finally resolved in favour of the latter by the collapse of the Mengistu regime, but remains intricately balanced even within the current political structure.

1   See *Adulis* (for the EPLF) Vol.1 No.11, May 1985; and *People's Voice* (for the TPLF), special issue "On our differences with the EPLF", 1986.
2   See, for example, Mohammed Hassen, *The Oromo of Ethiopia: A History 1570-1860*, Cambridge University Press, 1990.
3   See I.M. Lewis, *Peoples of the Horn of Africa*, London: International African Institute, 1955.
4   See K.E. Knutsson, "Dichotomization and Integration: aspects of inter-ethnic relations in Southern Ethiopia", in F. Barth, ed, *Ethnic Groups and Boundaries*, Bergen, 1969; see also P.T.W. Baxter, "Ethiopia's unacknowledged problem: the Oromo". *African Affairs*, vol.77 no.308,1978.
5   See A. Triulzi, "Nekemte and Addis Abeba: dilemmas of provincial rule", in D. Donham & W. James, eds, *The Southern Marches of Imperial Ethiopia*, Cambridge University Press, 1986.
6   See H. Blackhurst, "Ethnicity in Southern Ethiopia: the general and the particular", *Africa*, vol.50 no.1, 1980.
7   C. Clapham, "The Structure of Regional Conflict in Northern Ethiopia", *Cambridge Anthropology*, vol.13, no.2, 1989.

4 A New Beginning in Ethiopia and Eritrea: Guidelines to the Healing of the Land Through a Federal Structure

MARTIN DENT and ASFA WOSSEN ASSERATE

Ethiopia has suffered too much from the embittered and usually unnecessary quarrels of the last 30 years of her history. For the last five years or so of the rule of the Emperor she suffered an incipient guerilla war in Eritrea; for the next 17 years of revolutionary government she suffered from an unbroken series of wars and massacres in most parts of the country. Some of these were against and between various groups at the very centre of Ethiopia, and others arose from conflicts with movements of national or regional revolt in various parts of the country, or from the Somali invasion. Changes are not easy to make, and although a great deal of modernisation occurred under the late Emperor, other important changes, especially relating to land tenure, remained to be made. (The tragedy of Ethiopia was that at the moment when the greatest initiative was needed from him in 1970's he had become too old.)

In 1974 Ethiopia needed a revolution in the sense of a new beginning, a removal of certain feudal barriers and release of energy. What she got was a period of almost unbroken repression and state violence. There are those who preach the doctrine drawn not from Marx himself but from an inane neo-Marxism, that every revolution requires a civil war or a reign of terror. Ethiopia has paid in the blood of hundreds of thousands for the implementation of these repressive ideas. The necessary changes to land tenure and other structures were made quickly and with ease by the rural population themselves led by the students. They were accompanied by little violence and were complete before 1976 when the red terror began. The enforced abdication of the Emperor on 12 September 1974 and the overthrow of the imperial system was effected by a series of mutinies and demands of the military for change, combined with strikes and demonstrations by workers and students in large towns. No bloodshed had entered the process until on 29 November 1974, at

41

the height of the power struggle between Mengistu and his opponents in September 1974, Mengistu's supporters broke into the prison and slaughtered 60 of the senior servants of the Emperor's regime. This was not justice, for no evidence was presented against them, nor was it self-defence, for they were helpless prisoners at the mercy of their captors and with no armed supporters outside to help them; it was just a demonstration of revolutionary extremism expressing itself by gratuitous bloodletting, akin to the massacres of the Tuileries of the French Revolution.

Partly as a result of this atrocity and partly in reaction to the overthrow of the imperial system, there were revolts led by the old aristocracy and fiefholders of the late Emperor in several of the provinces in 1976, but these were speedily put down by the army. The invasion of Ethiopia by Somalia in alliance with the Somalis of the Ogaden, was decisively repulsed with Soviet and Cuban help in 1977 and then, just at the moment when the revolution would seem to have achieved secure victory over its external foes and over the old order, wholesale red terror was unleashed against Mengistu's revolutionary rivals.

The same total onslaught of violence, which was turned inwards against old servants of the state in Addis Ababa and against the Ethiopian People's Revolutionary Party and other left-wing rivals throughout the country, was also deployed against non-Amharic peoples and regions that sought for adequate expressions of local autonomy. The brief interval of hope for peace in Eritrea at the time of the accession of power of Amman Andom, himself half Eritrean, was swiftly succeeded by his assassination by Mengistu and by an all-out attack on Eritrean resistance fighters in the name of total and unmitigated power of a unitary revolutionary government. It did not enter into the conceptions of Mengistu's government to introduce the means of peace making and conciliation, for their style was always one of total violent onslaught against their foes and of an attempt to set up a system of total obedience dependent on coercion. Federalism and quasi-federal systems depend on restraint of government and the rule of law. These were at variance with earlier ideas of the total personal power of the Emperor, and therefore the federal status of Eritrea was unwisely removed in 1962. Federal ideas were even more at variance with the ideas of the 'Red Emperor', Mengistu Haile Mariam. The regime of Mengistu set up an academy for the study of the problems of the nationalities, and wisely ended the monopoly of Amharic in Government broadcasts and education.

It also proclaimed a doctrine of regional autonomy, but in the 1986 Constitution Ethiopia was declared to be a unitary state and all expression of separate identity of a political kind was ruthlessly repressed. The guiding principle of the newly established Marxist Workers' Party (WPE) which was intended to rule the People's Democratic Republic of Ethiopia, was one of rigid Democratic Centralism, where all decisions of importance were taken at the centre by Mengistu, the General Secretary of the Party and President of the Country and by his immediate associates. The country was divided in 1987 into five new autonomous regions and 24 new administrative regions in place of the former 14 provinces. These new structures did not amount to any effective form of federal devolution of a kind that might have helped to end the many separatist civil wars raging then. Tigrean and Oromo liberation movements were, likewise, unsatisfied with any overtures made by the Mengistu government, and the Somali resistance in the Ogaden threatened to come to life again in the absence of an adequate vision of a new federal Ethiopia on the part of the government.

Outline of a Future Federation

It was not possible, therefore, for a satisfactory peace to be attained under the Mengistu government, but it is our task here not to direct the argument *ad hominem*, or to the past, but to draw up a scenario for a harmonious federal settlement that might be achieved in the future. In doing this, we need to draw on federal experience elsewhere and to extend our conceptions beyond those used in the majority of settled federal systems, so as to find a way to satisfy the insistence demand of most Ethiopians to achieve '*Ethiopia tikdem*', (Ethiopia above all), through the preservation of its unity, while enabling Eritreans, and others who have fought for many years for sovereignty, to feel that they can achieve this goal within the framework of a new federal system for the whole country. This involves both the use of appropriate terminology, for words have vibrancy for politically interested people, and help to make a peace settlement acceptable, and also the provision of carefully thought out legal and governmental provisions for the flow of power in the political process of a 'New Ethiopia'.

First, as to terminology, we have to create new concepts. Eritrea will need to feel that it is sovereign, but at the same time it will have to be encouraged to form part of an 'Indissoluble union of the lands and peoples of Eritrea and Ethiopia.' If this sounds paradoxical we would reply that it is no more than the situation in which Britain is rapidly finding itself. Conscious of its own sovereignty, yet inextricably involved, (in fact if not in theory) in an indissoluble union of the EC under its accession to the Treat of Rome. We accept as a fact of political life in the EC that sovereignty can be divided and we find the arrangement workable and beneficial. The more theoretical objections of Alan James in his book *Sovereign Statehood,* (London, 1986) and others as to the divisibility of sovereignty do not interfere with the practical operation of the division of sovereignty involved in EC membership. If this is acceptable for a country of the importance of Britain, France, Germany or Italy, is there any reason why it should not be acceptable for a smaller country like Eritrea?

The sense of achieved identity in Eritrea, and among other peoples and lands in Ethiopia, can be enhanced by symbolic customs. Bavaria enjoys no special legal status in the constitution of the Federal Republic of Germany: in all the references it is just one of the eleven *Länder* mentioned together, yet as one drives to the frontier of Bavaria one sees a signpost proclaiming that you are about to enter the '*Freistaat Bayern*', (The free state of Bavaria). This is in a sense a kind of play acting, but it has invaluable political purpose. Together with a host of jokes and customs proclaiming the uniqueness of Bavaria, it proclaims a separate and satisfactory land identity, within the common loyalty of the German state. It is further expressed in a separate political party, the CSU, in alliance with the CDU, which is at present in power in the Federal

Republic, in fact it is a more or less integral part of the ruling party, but maintains a deliberate fiction of separateness. Other symbols are also important. Even in a unitary system such as Britain, Scottish banks can issue their own pound notes, (presumably under the strict control of the Bank of England), and these notes are legal tender. Similar licence could be allowed to Eritrea.

As regards the nomenclature of the future federation, the phrase 'Union of the States of Ethiopia and Eritrea ' or 'Union of the lands and peoples of Ethiopia and Eritrea' would convey the sense of a new social contract between peoples voluntarily entered into, but indissoluble as long as its basic compact is maintained and not violated by government. One cannot go back to the nomenclature of an empire, as in the old Ethiopian Constitution, nor to that of an imposed people's republic of a unitary kind as in the government of Mengistu.

Whether a name referring only to Ethiopia, or to Ethiopia and Eritrea, will suffice is not clear. Oromo, Tigreans, Somalis, Afars and other ethnic groups might consider themselves discriminated against in a title that referred to Eritrea but not to them. Clearly, there has to be an intense process of thought and discussion to arrive at the proper name for any new union. Perhaps one could speak of 'The Union of the peoples and lands of Ethiopia, Eritrea and the Horn of Africa' (though this would clearly imply the eventual inclusion of Somalia); alternatively one might copy the example of Ghana and Mali by resurrecting an ancient and prestigious name of an empire not entirely equivalent to the area of the new entity. 'Axum' as the centre of the ancient Ethiopian empire has resonance for Amharic and Shoa people, it also has the advantage of being geographically in the middle of Tigrean territory and very close to the Eritrean boundary.

Mengistu's government used the word 'Region' to describe the major component parts of Ethiopian and used the term 'Province' for much smaller units. 'Region' seems to us far too inert and geographical a term to have resonance or to inspire loyalty. 'Province' is better if applied, as it was in Imperial Ethiopia, to a major area. 'State' is also acceptable on the Nigerian, Indian or United States model, but perhaps the German word *Länder* anglicised as 'lands' conveys adequately the sense of an established and ancient entity existing in its own right, with a geographical base but also a call on the loyalty of its people, yet an entity not rivalry to the larger federal union to which it belongs. In African languages there are most frequent references to land in the sense of 'peopled land' (as in the Tiv saying *'arson'*, healing the relationships of the peopled land).

The Units of a New Federation

We come now to the constituent parts of the new federation. The fourteen provinces existing in 1980 - Arussi, Bale, Eritrea, Gemugofa, Gojam, Gondar, Hararge, Illubator, Kefaikaffa Shoa, Sodamo, Tigre, Wollega and Wollo might provide a base. The present 29 Regions might also form a starting-point, though the attempt in the new 1986 Constitution to break up existing entities such as Eritrea by creating ethnic linguistic states for Afar and Somali Issa people was unwise and unacceptable to the Eritrean and Tigrean liberation movements. An important principle of wise federal structuring is involved. Most successful federations use geography as a surrogate for ethnicity and avoid too much overt reference to tribe or ethnic identity . Thus in Nigeria there is a constitutional provision that one member of the cabinet shall come from each state. There is no statement that two members of the cabinet shall be Ibo or Yoruba, although Imo and Anambra states are solidly Ibo and Ogun. Oyo, Ondo and Lagos states are almost all (or predominantly) Yoruba. In Nigeria there are hardly any states accept for Akwa, Ibom and Bormo, that exactly correspond with an ethnic group, the others are either one of several states inhabited by a large ethnic group, or a state inhabited by a number of smaller tribes, like Bendel, Benue, Plateau, Cross Rivers, Rivers, and Kaduna. Thus one avoids paying to open a genuflection to ethnic identity since this tends to exclude from rights and belonging in the state those strangers of a different identity who live there. Ethnic and language groups tend also to be of different sizes and, therefore, it is difficult to give them each a state in federation of components of roughly equal size. Ethiopia, like Nigeria, has very many languages, it would be totally impossible to give them each a state or 'land'.

There is an additional advantage in a system where the states or *Länder* are or roughly equal size, as in Nigeria or in the 1980 Ethiopian provinces. It is going to be necessary in the new Ethiopia to take measures to prevent any group from feeling excluded from their fair share of the jobs and advantages of the country. Under the Emperor, for historical reasons, it was more difficult for a Moslem or a Somali speaker to achieve high rank in the imperial service or the army than it was for a Shoan or an Amharic speaker. Analysis of the composition of the ruling bodies under Mengistu shows that the imbalance remained. In a new Ethiopia built upon the voluntary support of all groups, each must feel that they are getting a fair share. As the Roman proverb has it *'Ubi bono, ibi patria'* ('where you feel well off, there is your fatherland'). Nigeria has dealt with this problem of spread of jobs and facilities by a doctrine of 'federal character'. As far as possible, jobs in the cabinet, in the army officer corps or in the federal civil service, are distributed equally between the states, while those available from the state government are distributed equally among local government areas in the state. As long as the sizes of the states and of the local government areas are of roughly equal area, this provides a rough approximation to equal and fair spread of jobs and government services.

The largest of the fourteen provinces in this list is Shoa, with a population of 5,864,000 of whom just over a million live in Addis Ababa. The Nigerian example may be worth following. Under the new constitution they have gone to great trouble to emphasise the fact that Abuga, the new capital, is not a state, but is federal territory available equally for the use of all Nigerians regardless of where they or their fathers were born. Addis Ababa should be federal territory and not a 'land' (or State). Even so, Shoa might need to be subdivided and Bale, Gemugoffo and Illubabor, all of which have populations under a million, increased in size. Alternatively, they could each be given half a share in distribution of federal posts, somewhat like a Swiss 'half canton'.

Mengistu's Ethiopian Constitution suggested a special status for the five autonomous regions. This has, however, considerable drawbacks. A working federation suggests symmetry among the powers and status of the component parts. Human beings tend to equate symmetry with justice and, therefore, it would be difficult to give one land or province powers which are denied to others.

A further element of federalism concerns local government. The federal way is not only a means of dividing power by constitution between two different levels of government, it is also a whole ethos of power sharing and of healthy autonomy, allowing people at a local level to look after those things that concern them at that level, while accepting the authority of the central government in those things which concern the country as a whole. It is therefore, altogether logical that in a federal system the areas, constitution and powers of elected local government authorities should be guaranteed. This was attempted in Nigeria by the famous 1976 Local Government Reform and is enshrined in the working of the new 1989 constitution. Elected local government councils and directly elected local government chairman are to be irremovable except by judicial trial or by impeachment for gross misconduct or by trial before the code of conduct tribunal. Their funds come direct from the federal government according to a 10% formulae of total revenues.

This kind of local government autonomy must be built into the new Ethiopian federal constitution for many of the units of traditional ethnic and linguistic identity in Ethiopia, which we wish to protect and foster, are too small for federal status as a 'land' or province.

The Division of Powers in a New Federation

We now come to the core of a future federal arrangement - the division of powers and the structure and operation of the authorities.

The first part of most constitutions concerns a statement of the source of power which in this case is the people of the whole of the union, we state the goal of the creation of a more perfect union of free 'lands' (or provinces) and then we go on to a comprehensive Bill of Rights. This is of paramount importance in Ethiopia today where people are conscious of continual invasion of their rights over the last 20 years or so. The Bill of Rights is properly a federal concern for the whole country. As in Canada, in the repatriated constitution the clear statement of fundamental rights is a key part of a federal power. As in Nigeria, we must set up a mechanism for the easy enforcement of those rights by direct access as of right to the High Court in each state. As in the United States, we shall find that the wording of fundamental rights provisions is of value in the political process and that whole structures of emancipation can be built upon a single phrase, as was done through the equal protection of the laws clause to put an end to racial segregation.

Among the rights guaranteed will, of course, be the freedoms of expression in every form, freedom from wrongful arrest and state violence. It has been characteristic of Mengistu's Ethiopia as of Stalin's Soviet Union, that elevated statements of constitutional or political right and liberation have gone hand in hand with actual murder of citizens by agents of the state in large numbers. There is no absolute constitutional guarantee against this for we can only protect the lives of citizens by a restrained, effective and law-abiding style of

46

government. We can, however, assist the process through the constitution. The 1989 Nigerian Constitution has, for the first time, introduced a clause that any death from police action or the action of the armed forces shall automatically be followed by an enquiry by an impartial body within a stated interval. Ethiopia could copy this provision. An institution as mundane as the inquest has in many places acted as a deterrent to those who are careless of human life.

Perhaps we could also go ahead of many states and expressly limit the death penalty to those convicted by judicial process of murder. Treason would then be punishable only by imprisonment. From St Thomas More to the victims of Mengistu the world is full of instances of people 'of whom the world was not worthy' who have been executed for treason. It is a category of alleged crime which, over the ages, has probably accounted for the lives of more innocent people in many countries than any other.

We are faced with a problem with regard to imprisonment. We must provide safeguards against prolonged imprisonment without trial, though, as the present Nigerian experience shows, a clause providing for release on bail after maximum of two months detention can be ineffective and numbers waiting trial may rise to half the prison population through the mere negligence and inefficiency of the authorities. Nonetheless, some constitutional provision to prevent prolonged imprisonment waiting trial is essential.

The state of the prisons themselves can be improved by an innovation in constitutional practice in the form of a mandatory regular inspection of the prison by a stated authority - a judge, administrative officer of senior rank of a prison visitor. It is also important to put an end to the Ethiopian practice, where prisoners are not fed but depend on friends and relatives outside to bring them food. This is tolerable for the rich and important, but dangerous and harsh for poor and ordinary people. One should not prohibit friends from bringing in food and other harmless items but a sufficient daily ration must be provided and this can be stated in the constitution.

The issue of preventative detention is a delicate one of great importance. Apart from the five years of Nigeria's Second Republic under Shagari from 1979 to 1983, no African state in recent years has been able to manage without a system of preventative detention. The scale of its use has, however, varied from the occasional in well run states, as in Nigeria under Gowon, to the excessive and tyrannical. We have to introduce a clause that will limit preventative detention to periods of emergency duly promulgated by the executive and legislature and provide for regular review of detainees by an impartial judicial authority.

Economic freedoms are hard to define in constitutional terms. Since the vast majority of the people of Ethiopia and Eritrea are poor, and since provision of essential amenities for them, including land to cultivate, has had so much attention in the promises of government and the aims of the revolution, we must include a statement on these lines, though this is likely to have to be in the nature of a 'Fundamental Objective and Directive Principle' (to quote the Nigerian phrase) rather than a justifiable statement. The old Ethiopian Constitution of 1955 contained an inspiring phrase that land is a 'sacred trust for the present and future of Ethiopia.' We must include and enforce such a provision. There must be no question of the restoration of the large estates expropriated and divided at the revolution for such a restoration would be politically totally unacceptable. The constitution could include a clause allowing the government to set a limit upon land holdings if it sees fit, though the Mengistu regime's 10 hectare limit is too low.

The freedom to buy and sell needs to be expressly stated, since one of the greater economic failings of the present regime has been to prohibit more successful farmers from selling their surplus grain on to a free market at a reasonable price. This has been a large contributory cause of famine and has been only partly modified under the pressure of the World Bank and IMF. Exact economic practices cannot be laid down in the constitution, nor would it be wise to make mention of any specific economic ideology, socialist or anti-socialist, but the basic freedom to trade and to set up enterprises, subject to regulation for safety, economic advantage of the whole community and avoidance of monopoly, needs to be stated in the constitution and will be much welcomed.

A clause for avoidance of expropriation of property without due legal process and fair compensation needs to be included, but the process of assessment of fair compensation often presents legal difficulty.

The next section in the constitution would most appropriately deal with citizenship and it is important that there should be a single citizenship for the 'Union of the lands of Ethiopia and Eritrea' with its attendant rights and duties. It may also be of advantage to have some legal category of citizenship of one of the 'lands' but this is not clear.

The most important section of the constitution of the new Ethiopia and Eritrea will deal with the constitution of the governing bodies and the division of powers between centre and lands. The central government must be elected, as must that of the 'lands' and of local government. If the task of ensuring fair elections, which command the confidence of all people in different political groups, is beyond the capacity of the internal resources of Ethiopia and Eritrea, it is permissible to supplement those resources by invoking the aid of an impartial outside body. This was done by Britain in the birth of Zimbabwe, it was done by the UN at the birth of an independent Namibia, it is done by bodies as jealous of their autonomy as the National Union of Mineworkers in Britain, who use the services of an impartial body, the Electoral Reform Society, to conduct their elections. A misplaced sense of national pride, until recently, prevented governments from making use of the services of outside bodies to conduct or monitor their elections. In fact, however, the conduct of an election is not an act of high policy and national sovereignty, but a mechanical non political function as mundane and demanding as the auditing of accounts, (as a function for which outside bodies such as Peat Marwick Maclintock or other international auditors are often called upon in many countries to officiate). It is a mechanical rather than a political function where a competent and impartial outside body has advantages over an internal one, which is likely to be subject to political pressures.

It is common in federal systems to have two houses, one directly elected by the people on constituencies delineated purely on numerical grounds (or grounds of local identity) throughout the country and the other, upper house, in some ways representative of the 'states', 'union', 'provinces', 'republics' or 'Länder' that comprise the federal system. This will be of value to us. It may well be that the Bundesrat of the German Federal Republic will provide the best model. It is a highly professional body, quite different in composition and style to the Bundestag, the lower house. Its members are directly appointed by the *Länder* governments and comprise both politicians and civil servants. The *Länder* Minister Presidents, the elected head of their governments, take the most important decisions, and when an issue arises of particular political difficulty they repair to a confidential meeting of eleven Minister Presidents in 'Room 13' before the main business of the Bundesrat begins. The West German, the Indian, the Nigerian and the Canadian Federal Systems, unlike that of the United States, make great use of the device of Executive Federalism, where the Head of Federal Government (or in the Nigerian case, the Vice President and President) meets regularly as part of the specified functions of government bodies, with the heads of the governments of the constituent parts of the federation. In Africa the politics of the 'big man' is of particular importance. The senior men must come face to face and arrive at acceptable solutions through discussions, if the business of government is to proceed in a satisfactory manner. The central government of the Union of the lands of Ethiopia and Eritrea will need to have adequate strength. The experience of Nigeria and of the United States before the civil wars is that an outward leaning federation did not suffice to hold the country together. As in India and in present day Nigeria or United States, one needs a strong and attractive federal government to preserve the peace and to seek to create the national identity. An inward leaning federation is, however, very different from a unitary system.

The head of the federal government will, of course, be elected either directly by the people or indirectly by the federal legislature. Either system is acceptable. Whether that headship of government shall be exercised by an executive president as in all African states except Morocco, Swaziland and Lesotho, or whether one could have some form of constitutional monarchy with effective political power in the hands of the Prime Minister, as in Britain or in Malaysia, is not clear. The monarchy had a very important roll in the history of the Ethiopian people, but it may be too late to seek to restore it as an institution, even in a constitutional form.

Judicial review will, of course, be another important element in the constitution for we have to replace arbitrary force by persuasion and by the regular operation of the laws.

What will be the powers of the various 'lands' under the new system? Clearly the role of the 'lands' cannot just be one of devolution, at the discretion of the centre. They are not to be regarded as a mere appendage of the central government for they will be, as we have argued, 'sovereign lands in a sovereign and indissoluble Union'. The 'lands' must have power to hasten their own development and must command adequate funds. Nigeria has arrived, after much anguish, at a revenue allocation formula which divides up the whole federally collected revenue and gives 32% to the states and 10% to local government as of right, the remainder is retained by the Federal government. Some such guaranteed revenue share written into the constitution of the 'Union of the lands of Ethiopia and Eritrea' will help to cement the settlement.

The division of subjects into exclusive federal (or union) concurrent subjects between centre and 'lands' and unspecified residue of subjects which are subject to the control of the 'lands' is easily managed on the pattern of federations such as the Nigerian or the Indian. There is also a need for the powers of local governments to be spelt out and guaranteed in the constitution for they are not to exist only at the discretion of the land or central governments.

Foreign affairs are, of course, a central responsibility as in every other federation, but the Union of Ethiopia and Eritrea could borrow from the West German practise in allowing 'lands' with the permission of the federal government to make agreements with foreign powers on subjects within the land jurisdiction.

The question of emergency is a vital one and presents a considerable problem. India has a constitutional provision allowing for the all Indian Government, with the ratification of Parliament to declare a state of emergency, called 'Presidential Rule', over a state, to suspend all the state political authority and replace it for a given period with direct administration from Delhi. This provision has often been used - probably too often! Nigeria seemed to have a similar provision in the Independent Constitution and this procedure was used by Alhaji Abubakar, the Federal Prime Minister, to take over the Government of the Western region during the First Republic. This intervention in state affairs was not repeated by Shagari during the Second Republic, despite considerable maladministration by several state governors. None of the federal systems in developed countries have this sort of wholesale power of intervention, though at times of war or emergency, federal governments have assumed important extra powers. The West German Constitution gives a specific right of the federal government to oversee administrative performance by the *Länder* in executing federal laws. On balance it would be unwise to have a specific emergency or 'Presidential rule' provision in a future federation encompassing the lands of Ethiopia and Eritrea. The component units would fear, with reason, that it might be used to undermine their federal status for political reasons. Some specific power of intervention in cases of breakdown of law and order or total administrative mal-performance is, however, desirable. Even a 'sovereign' state like Britain, for instance, can be brought before the European Court for failure to perform European Community obligations. In a full federation like that which we are proposing for Ethiopia and Eritrea, stronger sanctions will be needed.

The psychological factor will be all important in the process of building a new federation. Those who have fought long for their independence must feel that indeed the past has been thrown off. They have to know that the old imperial dominance is dead and the succeeding revolutionary dominance is dead. They have to see that what they are now creating is a voluntary union to which they give their assent, and that assent will be so much the stronger because it will be a free assent and not a forced one. They will be like the thirteen states' representatives who met in Philadelphia to form the 'more perfect union' of the United States in 1787, and like the state legislatures that subsequently freely ratified that constitution. We need, above all, a sense of a new beginning.

This is one side of the equation, but the other is equally important. Many, many people have fought and died in order to preserve the integrity of Ethiopia to give reality to the slogan *'Ethiopia Tikdem'*, 'Ethiopia above all.' They too must feel that the entity for which they have fought survives in its essence. The old forms, the old dominance will disappear, the Empire will exist no longer, the Mengistu dictatorship will exist no longer, and in its place will come the true union of hearts, the free and subtle institutions of an operative federal or confederal union. The long fight for the integrity of Ethiopia is not something that began in the last 30 years; it has been carried out against great odds, and in the end victoriously, for hundreds of years against those who have sought to submerge or break up the Ethiopian nation and the Ethiopian state. It was carried out by Theodosius, the Emperor who died by his own hand when he thought he had failed; it was carried out triumphantly by the great Emperor Menelik II; it was carried out heroically by Haile Selassie as he resisted the fascists invasion of Mussolini. It is, indeed, also a sacred cause.

We have, therefore, to bring together in one triumphant and voluntary union, those two causes that have been in conflict with much shedding of blood for the last 30 years. We have to create a new union that meets the aspirations of those who have fought for the freedom of their communities and the aspirations of those who have fought to preserve Ethiopia.

5 Eritrea: Prospects for Self-Determination

LIONEL CLIFFE

In the latter part of May 1991, the forces of the Eritrean People's Liberation Front (EPLF) defeated the Ethiopian army in a major battle some 50km south of the Eritrean capital, Asmara, which they went on to occupy. A Provisional Government of Eritrea (PGE) was set up in Asmara which has been administering the territory since mid-1991. Thereby, control of Eritrea by the Ethiopian Government in Addis Ababa was finally ended after thirty years of hard and bitter fighting. At the same moment, the rest of the army of the Ethiopian regime headed by Mengistu Haile Merriam was itself routed by the rebel forces under the Ethiopian People's Revolutionary Democratic Front (EPRDP), thus installing in Addis Ababa a government broadly sympathetic to Eritrea's bid for self–determination. The PGE planned a referendum for April 1993 in which the Eritrean people would be asked to vote on the issue of Independence, a status they overwhelmingly endorsed. This contribution will examine how this new status of *de facto* and unchallenged independence came about and what it portends for the future of Eritrea, and surrounding territories.

Eritrea's Past and Future Status

The area designated as Eritrea, consisting of a long, low-lying Red Sea coast littoral, the northern end of the highlands which also extend through Tigray and other provinces of Ethiopia, and plains extending into Sudan on the west, came under Italian colonial rule in 1890. It was the stepping-off point for the Italian fascists' invasion of Ethiopia in 1935, and like Ethiopia proper was 'liberated' by a British military campaign in 1941. Whereas control of Ethiopia was immediately handed over to a government under Emperor Haile Selassie, Eritrea was run by a British administration until 1951, while lengthy discussions were held in the post-war years about its ultimate 'disposal'. Various plans, including independence and division between Sudan and Ethiopia, became bones of contention between the great powers, with the USSR pushing for independence and the US inclined to pander to the whims of a Haile Selassie regime which was becoming a close ally. The eventual compromise adopted and guaranteed by the UN in 1952 was for Eritrea to have an 'autonomous' and elected government united in a federal relationship with the government in Addis Ababa - constitutionally a similar arrangement to that, at the time, between the governments of Northern Ireland and the United Kingdom, or was later to apply to the union of Zanzibar with mainland Tanzania. Relationships between the Asmara and Addis Ababa authorities were always fraught as the Emperor's emissaries continued to support campaigns for complete integration, and as they could never be constitutionally regularised, as is necessary to make any federal constitution workable, given the unconstitutional, authoritarian nature of the central government.

In 1961, the Emperor decreed the revocation of the separate, federal status of Eritrea and the disbanding of its government. Shortly thereafter armed resistance followed demonstrations against this incorporation, and continued for 30 years.

Ethiopian claims to Eritrea were based on two grounds. First the assertion of a common past based on a particular, and disputed, reading of several centuries of history, and a resulting shared culture. It is the case that the highland areas of south central Eritrea had often been locked into an interactive set of events and processes with the highland areas of Tigray and other parts of the old Ethiopian Kingdom(s), but these were as much relations of conflict as integration. These areas do share similar cultures - Coptic Christianity, farming systems and other characteristics - to a far greater extent than with areas of Southern Ethiopia which were absorbed into the empire by conquest only in the late 19th century. But such commonalities with 'Abyssinia' certainly cannot be read into the history and culture of the northern, western and coastal lowlands of Eritrea with their pastoral and agro-pastoral livelihoods, Islamic faith and quite different families of languages. Neither are the people in the south-west corner of Eritrea self-evidently 'natural' Ethiopians; any similarities in languages, faiths and history are with peoples of southern Ethiopia and northern Kenya and Uganda.

The second main claim for Ethiopia to cling onto Eritrea was that the federal union and its revocation in 1961 were not only legal acts but involved some process of self-determination by Eritrea. Specifically, they point to the active movement for 'Unity' that certainly did exist in Eritrea in the 1940s and the informed measuring of opinion by the British Administration in that period which did record some significant proportions (although based on a questionable 'sample') of opinion supporting union. The further evidence is put forward that in 1961 the Emperor's decree reversing the federal statutes did, in fact, receive the assent of the elected parliament in Eritrea. The counter-arguments put forward by Eritreans challenge not only the accuracy of the historical record but also its relevance. Common ethnic and cultural linkages and shared histories were systematically ignored in the creation of Africa's present, colonial borders. And yet, those states created by imperialism have been generally accepted as the basis for the independent nations of post-colonial Africa. The Eritreans point to the fact that from 1889 to 1935 and then again from 1942 to 1952, Eritrea had a separate legal existence within its present boundaries under first Italian colonial and then British military rule. They claim the same basis for current legitimacy as Ghana, Kenya or Zaire.

The Eritreans also contest the strength of the union movement in the 1940s and claim that the gathering of opinion and the final parliamentary vote in 1961 were the result of extensive manipulation by emissaries and officials from Addis and the Orthodox Church. The final parliamentary voting was certainly in favour; but the Eritreans point to its circumstances: the parliament being surrounded by tanks. Moreover whatever the extent of that support, it was restricted to highland, Tigrinya-speakers, who were nevertheless divided in this earlier period, with very minimal support among people away from the highlands who were predominantly Moslem and speakers of Tigre and other languages except for some of the peoples of the south-west.

These debates were the stuff of most discussions of the Eritrea question in the 1970s and 1980s, in political and intellectual circles in Addis Ababa and in Eritrea and in Africa and internationally, and no doubt historians and ideologues will continue to debate the correctness of the historical record and legal status. But in retrospect, it is pertinent to ask whether the energies spent on such issues were not only irrelevant but may have stood in the way of any resolution of the conflict. Implicit in the preoccupation with these claims was the assumption that the historical or legal claims could be settled beyond ambiguity and, moreover, that such unification could somehow remove the basis for conflict. The reality was that the interpretation of history was precisely a key element in the identifications and loyalties which were the basis for the conflicting nationalisms. Insistence upon such wrangles and the inevitable formulation of the problem in terms of 'rights' got in the way of any recognition of the appropriateness of compromise. It certainly prevented all influential circles in Ethiopia from realising that by the late 1960s, the highland peoples of Eritrea had rejected unionist ideas whatever the cultural and historical links - largely as a consequence of the generality and brutality of Ethiopian counter-insurgency methods. They were also incapable of recognising that by the mid-1980s the war was from all objective counts, unwinnable for the Ethiopians, as well as massively costly to the country's economy, budget and people. Thus, no realistic appreciation emerged that the conflict could only have been ended by negotiation and a political process, until the Ethiopian army's position had deteriorated to the point where it allowed an outright victory for the forces of Eritrean liberation.

The Eritrean counter-claim emphasised the legal dimension, arguing they are the one group of colonised people in Africa who have been denied any self-determination in the process of decolonisation. They argued that the allied powers' and UN's 'disposal' of the territory in a federation was done without formal consultations of the people and was against the wishes of the majority, and that the ending of Eritrea's federal status was unilateral. Moreover, they asserted that Eritrean's ex-colonial status means that theirs was not a case of 'secession' and did not infringe the principle of the inviolability of colonial boundaries espoused by the Organisation of African Unity (OAU). Their position should be seen as an exact parallel to that of the ex-Spanish colony of Western Sahara, whose annexation by Morocco (and earlier Mauritania) was challenged by the OAU and the UN. These arguments had been given some substantiation by international legal opinion (notably the International League for the Rights and Liberation of Peoples, 1980; and Fenet, 1988) which argued that earlier UN decisions have recognised the Eritreans as a 'people' with a consequent claim to decolonisation and self-determination, even though these 'rights' were agreed by the UN after the Federation. A further legal opinion strengthened this claim to self-determination by pointing to the fact that the UN's decision to promote a Federal Act contained international guarantees of the rights of the Eritrean people, which they lost with the end of the Federation and the UN's refusal to do anything but accept that termination. These considerations were at the root of the EPLF's proposals first made in 1980 for self- determination via a UN-monitored referendum.

Again it could be held that these legal postures are now academic given the *de facto* independence and observers' views about the widespread support for that Independence. But there are several reasons why these legal arguments still had a relevance to the Eritreans and to wider forces. For the EPLF and the Eritrean people a referendum would demonstrably establish beyond question the legitimacy of the shift to Independence. Such an outcome would give the final answer to sceptics who doubt the breadth of Eritrean nation-hood within the country. It would also have a significance within Ethiopia proper, undercutting the arguments of those who claim Eritrea, but also making it easier for Eritrea to be seen as a special case in terms of its legal status and thus without implications that would inhibit the preservation of some, consensual unity between other regions of Ethiopia. This kind of internationally recognised and constitutional process would reinforce Eritrea's legal claims and special status making it less of a worrying precedent for Africa and other OAU member states. The move toward an Independence sanctioned in this way would also make it easier for the international community to accept Eritrea as a member state, and thus bring many practical benefits to Eritrea (see below) and avoid diplomatic implications for UN member states.

The Liberation War: Its Character and Its Legality

There are many accounts from Eritrean sources and outsiders observing from Eritrean positions documenting the main battles and stages of the fighting, the organisation and tactics of the Eritrean liberation forces and some account of the effect of the long conflict on the people (Cliffe and Davidson, 1988; Sherman, 1980; Pateman, 1990; Yohannes, 1990; Cliffe, 1989)

- although there have been almost no detailed accounts from the Ethiopian side or using Ethiopian sources. In summary, these accounts set out the small, almost bandit-like beginnings of insurgency in the 1960s, the rapid build-up of an organised Eritrean Liberation Front in the late 1960s and early 1970s, from which the EPLF later split. They go on to record the mushrooming success of the two movements in gaining control over virtually all of rural Eritrea and most of the towns in the mid-1970s, and their subsequent reversal once the USSR provided military backing for the Ethiopian regime from 1978. There followed a period of stalemate from 1979 until 1984 with the EPLF forced into defending a small base-area in the north-centre of the country, mainly in the Sahel province, during which they repulsed several periodic Ethiopian offensives against their entrenched front line running south-west near the one town which remained under EPLF-control, Nacfa, which became thereby a symbol of Eritrean resistance.

The main legacy from that earlier period for today was the emergence of the EPLF and its later dominance over the ELF. The two movements indulged in two bouts of 'civil war': in 1972-74 which was ended partly by the intervention of Eritrean citizens appalled by the internecine violence and which left both sides intact, and then in 1981-82 during which the EPLF defeated the ELF and excluded their fighting forces from the territory itself. Since that latter date, the ELF has fragmented; one faction merged in 1987 with EPLF, others disbanded while some elements maintained an exile presence in Sudan and Arabian countries; the ultimate 'liberators' were thus the EPLF alone, which raises the question of whether the ELF exiles who have not returned in an individual capacity since May 1991 might command any public support in the country. This issue is ,in turn, related to the more general question of what the two fronts stood for, in terms of their policies and character, and the extent and location of their political support.

Controversies surround this latter question, although most commentaries (chiefly informed from the EPLF side even if not blatantly partisan) have tended to see the EPLF in the 1980s as embodying a more radical 'national liberation movement' with an agenda of social transformation and not just independence, and being more of a mobilising popular movement rather than the localised, patronage base which supposedly characterised ELF. There has also been a tendency to equate the Fronts with different ethnic and sectarian bases. But both radical-conservative characterisation of the differences, and that of Christian, Tigrinya-speaking highland agriculturalist support for EPLF versus Tigre-speaking, Moslem, lowland pastoralists behind ELF, are over-simplifications. Moreover, as far as any distinctions of orientation could be said to exist, there has been dispute about its possible causation: Pool (1986) arguing that it was only as the Eritrean liberation movement spread its support in the 1970s to agricultural areas with a more 'advanced' mode of production that it was able to break away from the narrow politics of patronage and bandit rebellion. On the other hand, Gebre-Medhin (1984 and 1989) argues that the roots of both movements were in the lowlands among agro-pastoralists, but that these communities had undergone a 'serf revolt', whereby former serfs had used the commercialisation of their livelihood under colonialism to partially emancipate themselves and sought to continue the process via the liberation struggle, thus providing an engine for radicalisation. Whatever the actual differences in origins and bases of the two fronts during the emergence and mutual confrontation, such bases for divisions may have little relevance in the 1990s, as their characteristics have changed. Such shifts have been most marked in the nature of the EPLF; notable here is not just the fact of its being the sole liberator but the manner whereby it shifted from its defensive position in the early 1980s to a successful offensive. The resistance to the Ethiopian 'offensives' of 1979-83 did of course include conventional, positional warfare and not just guerrilla tactics. The first shifts to an offensive capability occurred in 1984 with attacks in Barka province in the west which liberated some towns but only for a time, and then a surprise attack towards the northern town of Afabet in 1987 which breached and simultaneously outflanked the main Ethiopian trenches on the Nacfa front, thereby thrusting the two facing battle lines a 100 kilometres further south and east. The Ethiopians still commanded the highlands, including the capital, Asmara, and the mountainous terrain around the town of Keren which had been almost impenetrable (for instance for the British in 1940, and the ELF in 1975) and was seen militarily as the only entry point to the highlands.

The eventual final success of the EPLF was based on three surprising outflanking moves, each of which took time to set up. First, behind the screen offered by the front-line between Afabet and Keren, the EPLF built a new road, undetected, eastwards down to the coast, which enabled their forces a year later to mount a surprise attack to take the main supply port of Eritrea, Massawa. The control of the port cut off the main supply route for the Ethiopian army as well as providing much easier access to many areas for EPLF. From there, the final assault on the Asmara-Keren highlands triangle was eventually launched not from the difficult northern route through Keren, nor from the east up the steep escarpment between Massawa and Asmara, but from the south. This manoeuvre also necessitated construction of a new road southwest from Massawa into the southern part of the highlands. The first step in the final liberation involved EPLF taking control of the southern half of the highlands in 1989, thus putting them within 100 km. of Asmara. But this campaign also involved a major battle against a major Ethiopian military base further south in the province of Tigray, whereby joint forces of EPLF and their allies of the Tigray People's Liberation Front (TPLF) won a major battle and virtually gave TPLF control of the whole of their province. Not only was the Ethiopian army further weakened thereby, but it eliminated the possibility of attack by them or reinforcement of their army around Asmara.

These events led up to the final, major battles just south of the highland town of Decamhare in May 1991 which sealed the Eritrean victory. The Ethiopian army suffered major losses in the battle, withdrew its remnants to Asmara, while some attempted a retreat north and then west along the main highway toward Sudan - and only a few survived to give themselves up to the Sudan government. Others surrendered in Asmara and were then removed from Eritrea.

The nature of this strategy of the 1980s and the means whereby it was achieved testify to some of the capacities of the Eritrean liberation movement and isolating them helps to identify the potential legacy for a post-war Eritrea.

There was, first, an evolution of military capabilities from bandit groups in the early 1960s, to a guerrilla movement fighting a people's war in the late 1970s (after initial rapid successes and then reversals in the mid-1970s), to the emergence of a powerful conventional army able to win well-conceived campaigns in 'positional warfare' by the late 1980s. The final victories of the Eritrean People's Liberation Army (EPLA) and the EPLF's administration of a state in embryo in the liberated areas testify to a logistical and organisational capability. Their sappers and roadbuilders worked minor miracles and some considerable capacity for civil engineering and infrastructure building may result. These achievements were part of a broader process of generating a degree of technological self-reliance which may limit the degree of dependence in such fields as pharmaceuticals, health care, some mechanical engineering - even machine tools.

More generally, a self-confident 'can-do' mentality developed that will translate well into some tasks of the setting up and running of a new administration, especially in planning and organisation. One of the major successes of the EPLF was the running of the 'cross border' distribution of food relief from Sudan. This operation was more than just a mark of logistical effectiveness; it was a crucial element in their relationship with the rural people, especially of the west and north, areas that were 'liberated' for most of the 1980s. Popular support was a key element in their track record, as in all guerrilla struggles, and had certainly been in evidence before, but the famine relief distribution of the mid-1980s modified the patterns in several ways (see Pateman, 1988).

The dynamics of the interaction between the liberation movement and the people moved from passive support for political banditry, mainly restricted geographically to the north and west among predominantly Islamic, more livestock-oriented peoples, to a broad mobilisation where peoples from all regions contributed taxes, conscripts, intelligence and no doubt enthusiasm to a liberation army which provided increasing numbers of them with some protection, social and administrative services and, eventually, food. Up to the early 1980's popular support was differential between the two movements, the ELF which retained support in the north and west, and the EPLF whose cadres were mainly drawn from the highlanders: the Tigrinya-speaking, Coptic agriculturists who formed perhaps 45% of the population. Various outside observers have testified to the extent of and mechanisms for the mobilisation of a popular base (Leonard and other contributors to Cliffe & Davidson, 1988; Pateman, 1990). Other analysts have debated the possible explanations for the degree, timing and geographic and cultural nature of these popular bases of different movements. Pool(1981) suggests that the politicisation of the people could only be expected once the centre of gravity of the struggle shifted to an agricultural mode of production from the more 'backward' nomadic mode. Gebre-Medhin (1984) argues on the contrary that both fronts initially stemmed from the pastoral areas and that it was the changes wrought there by colonialism, and the partial erosion of aristocratic power there, which both provided a ready support for opposition to the backward step implied by overrule by a 'feudal' Ethiopian regime but which also stalled the further radicalisation because there had been partial social reform as a consequence of the 'serf revolt' of the 1940s and 1950s. Cliffe (1988) argues that the expansion of support into the highlands was not a 'given' but a result of specific initiative, notably a carefully orchestrated and popular land reform by the EPLF (and even in some places the ELF) in the late 1970s.

Whatever the contending explanations, what did change in the 1980s was that the EPLF through its Eritrean Relief Association (ERA) became the provider of food for the non-Tigrinya (agro-) pastoralists of the Sahel and Barka Provinces, areas that remained 'liberated' from the Ethiopian regime, but from which the ELF had by then been excluded. However, in the process the 'normal' relation between guerrillas who look to rural people to feed them had dramatically shifted: the people were now the dependants.

The then Secretary General of EPLF, Mohamed Ramadhan Nur, had in fact, made the observation in the early stages of the famine of 1983-85 that there was a possible danger of people's over-dependence on EPLF as it became a supplier of grain through the 'cross-border' operation from Sudan (interview, January 1983). As the famine's effects persisted and were amplified by the fighting, people in the liberated areas, which were expanding, continued to rely on this relief food, provided by donor agencies, distributed through the EPLF's relief arm, the Eritrean Relief Association (ERA). One consequence was the development of capabilities that impressed donors: a fleet of lorries, maintenance of roads, an effective and fair distribution network which reached people in their villages and thus kept them on the land and stopped their trek to famine camps, and so able to plant next year. This ability to deliver food, and also medical, education and other services was also instrumental in winning popular support, especially in the northern and western areas which were under EPLF control throughout the 1980s which had been more identified with the ELF in the previous decade. However, the operation also reversed the usual relation in this kind of struggle where peasants fed the guerrillas: the EPLF cadres showed themselves sensitive to people's urgent needs, but may have left a legacy of seeing them simply as objects of 'deliveries' rather than people engaged in their own forms of livelihood. There may be a continuing tendency to see those peasant systems of production as non-viable, encouraging the imposition of some outside, 'modern' alternative to replace them.

Such of course was the thinking behind earlier policy statements of the EPLF which declared that 'nomads' (which was how they referred not only to the 10% of rural households who were pastoralist but the 30% who were more accurately 'agro-pastoralists') should be 'settled' - a course which has been shown to be ecologically and sociologically inappropriate in much of Africa. Fortunately, a more pragmatic approach which backed off from settlement was spelled out in the 1987 Congress, perhaps so as not to upset the northern people politically. One hopes that such draconian measures will not reappear on the peace-time agendas.

Such issues will of, course, be among the many which have to be faced in mounting an operation of rapid recovery which began immediately after the May 1991 victory, and in confronting the eventual reconstruction and development. Most crucial of these transitional tasks is the provision *of food security*. The mutually reinforcing impact of drought and the laying waste of the countryside over a long period have seriously undermined the overall food producing capacity and the prospects of 'entitlement' to food on the part of an increasing number of impoverished rural dwellers. After the catastrophic drought years of 1983 and 1984, Eritrea has had adequate rainfall only in 1986: 1987 and 1990 were themselves drought years. There never was a long enough period for recovery, and that process was itself impeded by the war. Attempts have been made to gauge the additional impact of the succeeding stages of the conflict and of curfews, restrictions on trade and on movement of people and animals, and other repressive measures (Cliffe: 1989; ERD: 1992). Significant areas of arable land have been mined or lost to production by other means; surveys show that even areas of land pressure also suffer from a depletion of labour, especially of able-bodied adult males. But the harm done to the livestock economy and to the livelihoods of those dependent or raising animals and exchanging them for food are perhaps even more grave: their normal grazing patterns have been disrupted; beasts have been destroyed, maimed, confiscated; and normal access to markets, especially those in major towns was denied. There is strong evidence (ERD: 1992) pointing to a general impoverishment and depletion of resources in allowances. Food aid has helped to avoid deaths from hunger on a large scale but has not been enough to prevent a run down of productive assets; people have far fewer oxen than they need to plough; herds are too tiny to allow an annual off-take to provide even a bare living; the number of 'poor peasants' (roughly those who can survive by their own efforts on their own resources) has maybe increased from roughly 2/3 to 3/4 of rural households in the last five years.

This situation will require a continuation for some years to come of food aid, targeted so that it aids recovery. Even though 1992 was a year of unprecedentedly good rainfall, the long-term decline cannot be reversed at one go. A 'peace dividend' has been reaped in the months following May 1991 - normal trading has been resumed; some land has been reclaimed - but the rural areas have to recoup their oxen, herds and other assets and the process can be speeded up if food aid allows herds to be built up again without having to sell breeding stock for food. But in many other respects recovery of productive capacity will not be automatic or immediate. Indeed, there must be doubt about Eritrea's long-term capacity to be self-sufficient in food. The 1991 harvest was estimated to be sufficient for only roughly 15% of estimated grain requirements of the whole population for the following year - although that was a year of poor but not disastrous rainfall coming at the end of the long decline. With a degree of recovery, that half of the rural population living in the highlands might approach levels of overall production to meet its net grain requirements; parts of Seraye Province might even produce a net surplus. The 40% of the rural population living in more marginal areas and dependent on a more mixed, 'agro-pastoral' means of livelihood are probably only going to approach subsistence levels in the one year of really good rainfall occurring every five years. With an urban population making up a high and growing proportion, 30%, of the total population, plus over half a million refugees and exiles likely to return, the prospects of meeting staple food needs are remote.

This consideration must be one of the central issues in formulating an overall strategy for economic reconstruction and development: how to pay for imports of food and other necessities, plus equipment and materials for the sizeable industrial sector and for infrastructure? There are only small, presently workable deposits of minerals, but perhaps some limited long-term potential for further development of raw material exports. The industrial sector did constitute perhaps a third of the total manufacturing capacity of the larger Ethiopia. It was virtually all closed down during the war, but efforts were made from mid-1991 gradually to rehabilitate the factories and seek spare parts and sources of raw materials, especially for textiles, and some were back in production by the end of 1992. Using whatever unknown source of finances, the workers in these former state-owned factories were kept on the pay roll after the Provisional Government came to power until they reopened. Whether this existing plant, rather than new enterprises, can be the target of stated policies to promote partial privatisation of the economy is not clear. The only sources of investitive capital that have so far indicated any interest in bringing in funds are some international businesses run by Eritrean exiles. However, their resources are limited, and if their activities are confined to the take-over of existing publicly-owned businesses, this might off-load some of the chores of rehabilitation from the new, over-burdened state structures, but will not provide any additional productive capacities.

The Politics and Administration of the Transition

The body primarily taking on board these issues is a Provisional Government of Eritrea (PGE) set up immediately after the EPLF forces entered Asmara. The structure of the PGE as a whole was an amalgam of the established Departments of the EPLF with the former ministries of the Ethiopian-run administration. Ethiopian officials were expelled along with the remnants of the army, but all Eritrean civil servants, who occupied all the various levels of administration apart from the most senior executive levels, were kept on and guaranteed their posts and salaries. Virtually all decision-making posts were filled by senior EPLF figures. They and EPLF cadres brought in at the more middle levels were to remain as 'volunteers' during the two year interim, most living in camps and barracks receiving free board and a little spending money but no salary. Several individual Eritreans who had been living abroad and were not associated with the EPLF and its 'mass organisations' overseas, including some former ELF members, returned to broaden the political composition of the administration. By mid-1992 some of the factions of the former ELF, or their leaderships, had formally resolved to dissolve and to bring their members and resources under the PGE. The head of one of these, ELF-United Organisations, stated in May 1992 that the 'PGE's commitments to give the country a multi-party political system meant that there was no longer any valid reason to justify the continued presence of Eritrean liberation movements abroad'. Two members of the ELF-UO were subsequently appointed to the five-person Committee set up to prepare a referendum in April 1993.

The referendum represents the realisation of something first proposed by EPLF in 1980. Its oft-stated bargaining position was this proposal for an internationally supervised referendum which would freely allow Eritreans to choose between three options: independence, the revision to the federal status of the 1950's, or union with Ethiopia. This offer did win the EPLF a degree of international respect if not much support, but negotiations were consistently refused by the Ethiopian government. There was a *de facto* separate status in Eritrea from 1991 and a unilateral declaration of independence was not only possible in 1991 but was clearly a tempting prospect. But very quickly after the PGE was formed, it declared there would be a two-year interim and then a referendum. Among the reasons was clearly the desire to be seen to be consistent and to demonstrate, particularly to a still sceptical outside world, an independent state's claim to legitimacy. The PGE leadership also stated that another factor, and one that led to the relatively long period of transition, was a tactical ploy to avoid complicating emotions being aroused in Ethiopia proper during the very sensitive negotiations to set up a unified but decentralised state there. In the event, two years was still not long enough for the UN to agree to supervise the referendum. So in mid-1992, the PGE announced that it would go ahead with the setting up of a supervisory Committee, whose composition is relatively neutral,[1] to hold a referendum in April 1993, with the UN and other international actors being invited to send observers. The PGE's plan simplified the options and the question on the ballot was a straight yes or no about Independence.

The period up to the referendum marked a very distinct transition. The result of the voting was all but a foregone conclusion, so formal Independence almost inevitably followed. In the meantime, however, the status which Eritrea enjoyed in the international community of states was ambiguous and the absence of formal international recognition of Eritrea affected some crucial aspects of everyday life. Unable to join the International Telecommunications Union immediately, telephone and other links to the outside world were not put in place for some 15 months after May 1991. A postal service with the outside world also took time to set up. For similar reasons, the commercial banks in Eritrea which were separated off from the Ethiopian state-run commercial bank were not accredited for foreign exchange transactions. and thus international payments could only be transacted with difficulty - although payments in, of remittances for instance, were accepted gratefully and without fuss. This was part of a more general monetary difficulty: not only was the form of currency still the Ethiopian *Birr*, that has a fixed exchange rate to the US dollar (roughly 1B=$1), it also arguably represented what economists call an 'over-valued' currency. Thus Eritrea faced constraints from following much independence in its monetary policies, although they did not prevent the PGE from offering a differential rate, twice the official one, to the Eritreans who were repatriating foreign exchange.

The territory's ambiguous international status also inhibited diplomatic and aid ties with other countries. During 1991, most donor agencies seemed willing to provide emergency aid, especially relief food which was certainly badly needed following the drought year of 1990, but were reluctant to contemplate development aid. The major western governments took slightly varying positions: the US was the first to signal an interest in moving toward diplomatic relations; the British after some initial hesitation also followed the logic of an inevitable independence and began to lay the foundations of normal diplomatic ties. The PGE took exception to what they saw as the French role of using their influence and military presence in Djibouti to promote a dissident movement among the Afar people, who are found in the south-east of Eritrea, in Djibouti and in the coastal parts of Tigray and Wollo provinces of Ethiopia, to promote their separate political existence. These disputes were apparently resolved in January 1992 when an official French delegation was received in Asmara.

Relations with western powers, at least, and other linkages with the outside world were made more complicated by a conscious stance of the PGE. Although relationships with the new Ethiopian government were close, the PGE made it a matter of principle not to deal with the outside world through Addis Ababa. They refused to receive officials of embassies in Addis Ababa; they refused to have aid needs requested and met as part of an Ethiopian country programme. There was certainly a cost to this insistence that they no longer be treated as an appendage of Ethiopia, in terms of great inconveniences and of the reaction of outside governments to this upset of their formal protocols and programme hierarchies. But by 1992 most governments had adjusted to the realities of Eritrea's *de facto* separation and to the inevitability of its eventual independence: external communications and most diplomatic relations had been normalised, and long-term aid was in the planning stage.

But this 'take-us-or-leave-us' attitude still persists. It is symptomatic of a surprising limitation in the EPLF; for a movement which has been so adept, effective and adaptable in many respects, its consistent shortcomings in diplomacy and international public relations compared with other liberation movements that have achieved less on the ground are difficult to explain. Perhaps they are the legacy of enforced self-reliance without significant international backing and a strategy that believed action within the country was what mattered. Whatever the explanation, a recent, reported statement by Issayas Afeworki illustrates the attitude: 'On the question of whether we will lose recognition if the UN does not participate [in supervising the referendum]. it is not within the power of the UN or any other force to give its blessing to the outcome of the referendum ... It is the wishes of the Eritrean people that will decide the issue'. Here, the running together of the referendum result with the 'recognition' issue glosses over the fact that 'recognition' means, by definition, acceptance by others; it means being voted in as a member of the international club of states, an invitation more likely to be proffered as a result of a degree of courting rather than a terse presentation of credentials, however strong they are.

One area where this fence-mending still has to be done is in Africa. In past decades, OAU members bought the Ethiopian argument that the Eritrean movement represented not self-determination as in the comparable case of Western Sahara, but 'secession' (for the contentious nature of this position see Fenet, 1988), a notion that seemed to set dangerous precedents for many African regimes.[2] Some lingering unease about accepting Eritrea's *de facto* existence as a state seems to persist in OAU circles, despite the fact that the Ethiopian and Sudanese regimes support it, and the fact that bilateral relations have been forged with Kenya and Egypt. Thus in June 1992, the OAU foreign ministers rejected the PGE's request even for observer status at the next OAU summit. However, at a more concrete level, Eritrea has been accepted: the University of Asmara into African Universities circles, for instance. The OAU stance is not a major drawback in terms of resources and *real-politik*, but could influence diplomatic processes *vis-a-vis* the UN which tends to invite OAU opinion on matters African.

Relations in the Horn of Africa

For Eritrea the relationships which matter most immediately, in addition to trade, aid and communications with the developed countries, are those with Ethiopia and Sudan, with which it has common borders, and to some extent Somalia, Djibouti and Kenya, and the states just across the Red Sea. As noted above, the EPRDF-led government in Ethiopia accepts the case for Eritrean self-determination. There is close contact between the two. The PGE has a liaison office in Addis Ababa. The EPLF was not officially represented at the round table conference on 'peace and democracy' of all Ethiopian movements in Addis Ababa in July 1991, but did have observer status and still remains in touch with not only the EPRDF but other movements. Indeed, there are those, mainly supporters of the old form of unified Ethiopia (and usually of either the Haile Selassie or Mengistu regimes) who see a conspiracy at work: seeing the TPLF, as the dominant force in EPRDF, as ethnically and ideologically indistinguishable from the EPLF, and the two movements as having a common strategy, which is variously suggested as the splitting away of Tigray from Ethiopia and its union with Eritrea to form a state dominated by Tigrinya-speakers, or their common dominance of Ethiopia-Eritrea as a whole. Apart from the obvious illogicality of setting up a separate Eritrea if the latter is the long-run aim, there were complications in the past relations between TPLF and EPLF, and between Eritreans and other movements that make such a simplistic scenario improbable.

EPLF relations with TPLF were marked by alliance and collaboration, but also at times by discord. Throughout most of the 1980s the two movements did make common cause and co-ordinated their strategies in fighting Mengistu's army, and the last decisive battles of 1990 and 1991 in the two theatres were partly orchestrated. However, there was also a period of antagonism in the second half of the 1980s. The TPLF, particularly with the emergence of a Tigrayan Marxist tendency during which an ultra-left element identified with Albania, did develop a critique of the EPLF as 'bourgeois' and 'pragmatic'. At the same time, the TPLF was critical of the apparent shift in EPLF's war aims from regional autonomy to independence. In fact, from the mid-1980s when eventual independence for Eritrea became a real possibility, EPLF strategy, while still asserting its own demand for complete autonomy, also articulated a concern to avoid a complete break-up of Ethiopia proper under the centripetal pressure of the several movements of 'nationalities' and urged them to make common cause around the objective of defining a different and more federal central authority in Addis Ababa. In pursuance of this strategy, the EPLF sought to promote close links with other movements such as the Oromo Liberation Front, the Sidamo Liberation Front, the Afar Liberation Front - all of which sent fraternal delegates to the EPLF's Second Congress in 1987, which the TPLF did not attend. The EPLF's concern was to prevent a total breakdown of all authority in Ethiopia proper, which would have been a recipe for continued conflict which would impinge on Eritrea whatever its status, and also provide an invitation in what was still the era of cold war politics, for the US to intervene to replace the USSR.

In the event the TPLF was persuaded, through what processes is not known, to take on these broader goals, and it did form the EPRDF alliance. But through this process of concerning itself with the several national movements in Ethiopia, the EPLF also found itself in a situation of some complexity after the fall of the Mengistu regime. As tensions mounted between the EPRDF and the OLF in early 1992, and clashes occurred and the latter refused to participate in regional elections, the EPLF was in an ambiguous position given that ties with the OLF, and with other movements in Ethiopia, were at least as close as those with the EPRDF. In the end, the EPLF sought to use its good offices to try and reconcile the parties and involved itself in a tri-partite commission to run the postponed elections in Oromo areas.

Close ties were also established from the outset of the PGE, with the military government in Sudan. In fact the three governments of Eritrea, Ethiopia and Sudan made a joint declaration forswearing interference in each other's internal affairs and seeking to reduce outside intervention in the Horn. The previous years had of course seen a pattern whereby each government used support for rebel movements next door as a lever against the other states: Mengistu backed the SPLA in Sudan - and movements in Northern Somalia; different Sudanese regimes provided varying amounts of support to the Eritrean liberation movement, at least sanctuary and a route for food. At the same time, the EPLF, as we have seen, gave backing to several nationality movements in Ethiopia. This pattern has, for the moment, been reversed. For a variety of reasons, to do with the terrain, with the dominant position in Ethiopia of an EPRDF which has vouchsafed designs on Eritrea, the absence of a strong army in Addis Ababa, there is little basis for or prospect of interference in Eritrean politics from Ethiopia. However, the lowlands around two sides of the border area with Sudan, and the ethnic, cultural and religious ties of peoples in the north and west of Eritrea, could give Sudan greater potential leverage in future. Although there is a strong unity in Eritrea at present, the potential for cleavage along ethnic-religious lines must always be kept in mind. Thus the emergence of a small Eritrean movement, Jihad Islamiyya, in the border areas in the late 1980s was a significant irritant to the EPLF. This Islamic organisation did receive support from the increasingly fundamentalist regime in Khartoum, even into the second half of 1991, and did mount some minor sabotage and ambushes from eastern Sudan into Eritrea (HAB, 3, 1992). However, the regional alliance paid off for the PGE, in terms of *real-politik:* in the wake of some successes against the SPLA, the Sudan government rounded on the Jihad Islamiyya, destroyed its training camps in eastern Sudan and sent its leaders into flight into Saudi Arabia.

The Sudan government and PGE also considered joint action over Somalia. They were involved together in trying to mediate in late 1991 and early 1992, and even contemplated sending in a joint peace-keeping force - a reflection of a common desire for the region to seek its own solutions rather than rely on major power intervention, and of the fact that the end of its war in 1991 left the Eritrean army as one of the most formidable and certainly most disciplined military forces in the Horn.

However, the two governments are not 'natural' allies. In the long run, it remains to be seen how far the current 'live-and-let-live' stance and the making of deals which benefit both sides in immediate terms are sufficient to overcome the great ideological division between the growing Islamic fundamentalism in Khartoum and the determinedly secular, multi-ethnic movement in Eritrea. Much will depend on the kind of politics that emerges in the promised multi-party system of post-referendum Eritrea (see below).

Underlying the logic for political ties in the Horn are economic arguments. There was a gradual realisation on the part of the EPLF even before 1991, that the well-being of the Eritrean economy depends on trade and other ties with other countries. For so long, one argument the Ethiopian regime advanced for hanging onto Eritrea was access to the sea. The fear was fuelled that once in control of its ports, an independent Eritrea would have a stranglehold over land-locked Ethiopia. While this could be true in theory, it ignores the realities. The hinterland of Eritrea's main port, Massawa, consists of Eritrea itself and only the Tigray province of Ethiopia, with which Eritrea needs to trade, for food especially, and potentially parts of eastern and southern Sudan. The southern Eritrean port of Assab is the life line for Addis Ababa and most of Ethiopia. But that port serves no populous part of Eritrea itself, so the only economic benefit to Eritrea stems from it busily playing its role as entrepot for Ethiopia. The mutual benefit in getting the port rebuilt after damage in the late stages of the war and working to full capacity was recognised by an agreement that Assab be a free port for Ethiopia's goods.

More generally, the Eritrean economy's reliance on food imports for the foreseeable future, its significant industrial capacity, once factories are reopened, (perhaps 30% of all the manufacturing industry in Ethiopia in the past), the technological savvy of its people, and its long Red Sea coastline, all are factors dictating the need to foster a trading economy with close and open ties with Ethiopia especially, and with other neighbours including those in Arabia. Eritrea will also depend centrally on foreign exchange remittances from its migrants throughout Ethiopia, in eastern Sudan, in the middle eastern oil states and beyond. So friendly ties which at least avoid a sudden exodus back into Eritrea are also crucial.

Other aspects of regional economic co-operation would also be useful for Eritrea: relative freedom of movement for pastoral herders as well as migrants would enhance survival mechanisms for many in Eritrea and elsewhere; the potential services to the environment represented by regional organisations, like the new Intergovernmental Agency against Desertification and Drought (IGADD) and the old Desert Locust Control Organisation.

Eritrea after the Transition

Predictably, there was an overwhelming vote for independence in the 1993 referendum: there was a 98.5% turnout, of whom 99.8% voted yes, and thereafter a fully-fledged Eritrean government came into existence which received recognition internationally, even if with some lingering reluctance in parts of Africa. But although some pronouncements have been made about future political arrangements, the general picture remains opaque. The EPLF committed itself at its Second Congress in 1987 to a multi-party democracy. It has also restated its view that its task as a 'national front' will have been achieved with 'liberation' of the country and that it will cease to exist after the referendum. But it is hard to discern the outlines of a political system which might emerge - the potential shape of parties but also the broader contours of civil society. Although all individuals and groups (presumably informal ones) who take any position on the referendum have been assured the freedom to campaign, no political parties even in embryo are contemplated in this interim - and few initiatives seem to be contemplated. Issafas Afeworki gave it as his opinion in May 1992 (HAB, 3, 1992) that regulations should prohibit political parties based on religious, ethnic or provincial ties - it is not clear whether this was also the view of the EPLF Central Committee which held its fifth session at this time. The avoidance of such political identities with their potential for patronage politics and, given Eritrea's cultural and ethnic make up, even polarising disruption is understandable. But to do so by legislation does also remove the possibility of a mutually agreed confederal agreement between nationalities which the EPLF, correctly perhaps, sees as the best solution to imposed centralism in Ethiopia. But will outlawing such policies of free expression, even of ethnicity, make them go away? Could they not smoulder away untreated, or emerge in other guises as in Nigeria?

What alternative pattern of politics is envisaged or is feasible? Presumably the implication is for political parties to emerge based on interests and/or ideology. So far it seems to be imagined that these will spring from the ground in the immediate aftermath of the transition. But how? There is no indication as to whether a party or several will emerge from within the EPLF itself. It is unlikely that all of its activists will choose political retirement. Will leaders of discernible groups try to retain its mantle? Clearly there is a risk that if the EPLF or the present PGE took too much of the initiative to orchestrate the political parties, the emerging system could be seen as too stage-managed, and the process of former ELF and other opponents coming in from the cold could be reversed. But there is also a risk from all debate about the future shape of politics and policy being put on hold throughout the transition. As elsewhere in Africa, any genuinely free and competitive political system will depend on the emergence of vigorous groupings, many informal, and more general social and cultural interaction. Some elements of such a popularly-based civil society are an important legacy from the long-struggle - the determination, the organisational and technical creativity, the flexibility. But time for the emergence of pluralist views, of debate and compromise to emerge from the shadow of the effective but disciplined movement for liberation are also required. The transition would have been a potentially fruitful period for encouraging a general climate of discussion about the future, fostering the formation of that civil society and even embryo political groupings, but the start of that informal process has been for the moment postponed.

---

[1] The Chair was an Ethiopian diplomat until 1985, with OAU experience, before becoming an academic in the US; the others included two former ELF-UO members and two lawyers in private practice.

[2] Symptomatic of how this view persisted, was the position ex- President Nyerere took when he was considering accepting the role of co-chair with ex-President Jimmy Carter of belated peace talks over Eritrea in 1990. In prior meetings with the EPLF, he sought to measure their willingness to negotiate by getting them to agree in advance to drop demands for complete independence. Keen as he undoubtedly was to promote peace, he nevertheless was not prepared to see the issue of one of self-determination, or to accept the premise of talks without preconditions. (Interview with EPLF negotiator, Abdemichael Kassai, Asmara, September 1991).

References

Cliffe, L. & Davidson, B., eds. 1988, *The Long Struggle of Eritrea for Independence and Constructive Peace* (Spokesman, Nottingham).

Cliffe, L., 1989, 'The Impact of War on Different Agrarian Systems in Eritrea' *Development and Change*, Vol 20, No 4.

ERD (Emergency Relief Desk) 1992, *Eritrea 1992: A Needs Assessment Study*, by Centre for Development Studies, University of Leeds.

Fenet, A., 1988, The Right of the Eritrean People to Self-Determination', in Cliffe & Davidson.

Gebre-Medhin, J., 1984, 'Nationalism, Peasant Politics and the Emergence of a Vanguard Front in Eritrea', *Review of African Political Economy*, No 30.

Gebre-Medhin, J., 1989, *Peasants and Nationalism in Eritrea: A Critique of Ethiopian Studies* (Red Sea Press, Trenton).

International League for the Rights and Liberation of Peoples, 1980, *The Eritrean Case, Proceedings of the Permanent People's Tribunal,* (Milan, May, 1980).

HAB, *Horn of Africa Bulletin* (bi-monthly, Uppsala, Sweden).

Pateman, R, 1988, 'Drought, Famine & Development' in Cliffe and Davidson.

Pateman, R., 1990, *Eritrea: Even the Stones are Burning* (Red Sea Press, Trenton).

Pool, D, 1980, 'Revolutionary Crisis and Revolutionary Vanguard: The Eritrean People's Liberation Front', *Review of African Political Economy*, No 19.

Sherman, R., 1980, *Eritrea: The Unfinished Revolution,* (Praeger, New York).

Yohannes, O., 1990, Eritrea: *A Pawn in World Politics,* (University of Florida Press, Gainesville).

6 Eritrea: the Economic Challenge

PAUL B HENZE

An important chapter in Eritrean history has come to a close. The Derg's brutal 16 year campaign to subjugate Eritrea by military force has come to an ignominious end. Failure in Eritrea is a critical aspect of the failure of the Derg's program for orienting Ethiopia toward the Soviet Union and locking the country into rigid communist rule. Communism brought unmitigated disaster on Ethiopia and the Horn of Africa, as it has to all other parts of the world where it has been imposed. It is now collapsing everywhere and survives only in China, Cuba, and a few other political backwaters. The collapse of communism is not the end of the story, however. An encounter with Marxism-Leninism leaves a legacy of severe political, economic, and social problems, as we see in the newly democratising countries of Eastern Europe and in the rapidly disintegrating Soviet Empire. Though all but communist party functionaries and other direct beneficiaries of communist regimes welcome their demise, there can be little time for rejoicing. Everyone must go to work to repair the damage. Liberated societies face urgent new problems. If these problems are not dealt with successfully, the damage Marxism-Leninism has caused will be extended and compounded.

The revolution communists claimed to be implementing has been overtaken by a worldwide surge of commitment to democracy and pluralism. In contrast to communists and advocates of other forms of authoritarianism, those who practice democracy do not claim to be able to devise perfect political and economic systems. They recognise that individuals and societies are not perfectible, only manageable and improvable. Democracy requires leaders, but it also requires that leaders be accountable to their people and be reconfirmed or changed periodically by peaceful procedures i.e., elections that offer real choices. Democracy is a method for accommodating diversity and coping with change. A democratic system requires interplay and competition among economic, social, and intellectual forces and accommodation of ethnic and religious differences. Pluralism is an essential feature of democracy. Democracy is a system of majority rule but it must provide protection for minorities or it is untrue to its basic principles and ceases to be democracy. While adherence to all these basic principles is essential for real democracy, there is no single set of rules and procedures that can be applied to create and maintain a democratic political system. Every democratic system is an ongoing experiment in self-determination and government by consent of the governed.

Democratic systems can fall into crisis. They need periodic adjustment, but they have a capacity for self-correction superior to all forms of authoritarianism. The greatest advantage of democracy—which the history of the 20th century has demonstrated—is that over time democratic societies have been more successful than others in generating material progress, economic modernisation, and constructive social change.

Everything I have to say here takes recent worldwide historical developments into account. I have not changed the judgments on the relationship of Eritrea to Ethiopia and the rest of the region which I have expressed over a period of several years in many publications, so I do not repeat them here.[1]

Current Realities

It is even more urgent for Eritreans to leave arguments about the past aside and give priority to the future, for it is in their hands. Ethiopia's experience with communist militarism was so devastating and disillusioning that the country must be reconstituted as a kind of federal state to be able to survive at all. If the Derg's armies which benefited from more than 12 billion dollars' worth of Soviet arms could not subjugate Eritrea (or Tigre, or other parts of the country that escaped Derg control), no foreseeable government in Addis Ababa is going to be able to impose its will on the country by military force. No major foreign power is likely to be interested in intervening in the region. The Eritrea of the future will not need to protect itself against dangers that no longer exist. Ethiopia (and all Horn countries) will have to be governed in the future by a high degree of consensus based on compromise if they are to be governed at all. If no foreign power supplies weapons (extremely unlikely), there can be no possibility of imposing central government authority by force. Eritrea's autonomy—its right to self-determination in the sense of self-rule—is thus no longer at issue. The future is in the hands of the leaders of the Eritrean struggle and Eritrea's people. They can manage it well or badly. It is their responsibility. If an open, democratic society can be created in Eritrea, Eritreans stand a fair chance of developing a flourishing economy that will benefit the entire region.

Not so many years ago leaders of insurgent movements appeared to be offering Eritreans only two choices: (1) to join the Arab world or (2) to become an Albania on the Red Sea. Both were so unpalatable to many Eritreans that the Derg seemed a lesser evil. The insurgent movements originally gave no priority to economics. Nevertheless, many Eritreans—traditional traders from ancient times—ignored dogma and made the best of a bad situation. Some moved abroad and sent money home. The majority who remained in Eritrea created an underground economy that served elementary needs of the people and maintained links with the entire region. The Derg never felt strong enough to attempt to impose its total economic design on Eritrea. Mengistu relied on an endless flow of Soviet weaponry to solve all problems. Gradually, insurgent leaders evolved in their own perceptions of the world. Life was maintained in Eritrea in spite of severe handicaps. Starvation was averted by local exertions and food from abroad. With all this, however, Eritrea only managed to exist, not prosper, for more than two decades. With the end of the struggle for self-determination, Eritreans' expectations for rapid improvement in their situation are rising rapidly.

Urgent Tasks

Economic challenges are more urgent than political issues, though there is a direct relationship between the two. Urgent economic tasks include:
• Feeding the population and providing elementary needs: water, fuel, clothing, medical supplies, etc.
• Bringing the underground economy to the surface: restoring trade, crafts, and basic services.
• Extending and restoring utilities and transport.
• Activating industries which are capable of producing consumer goods, and, as soon as possible, exports.
• Restoring banking facilities and maintaining dependable financial arrangements.
• Implementation of a revenue system to support local and regional government services.
• Re-establishment of the legal framework necessary to sustain a flourishing private economy.

Eritreans are eager to help themselves but need assurance that their efforts will be rewarded. To be encouraged to produce maximally, farmers need to be able to sell freely and at a profit. Markets need to be free and open. Farmers need to feel secure in use of their tools, animals, and land so they will invest and raise productivity. State farms create inefficiency and waste. Most should be turned over to other forms of ownership. Commercial agriculture has a proven potential in Eritrea. Rapid restoration of confiscated agricultural estates to their original owners or other private operators will have a beneficial effect on the entire economy and will encourage new foreign investment. Enterprising Eritreans should be encouraged to expand commercial agriculture.

For a long time, unemployment will be a major problem in Eritrea. People in both rural areas and towns will need opportunities to work and earn. Hindrances to trade and practice of crafts should be removed. Eritrea still possesses one-third of Ethiopia's industrial base. It should be got back into operation as soon as possible and arrangements for privatisation of ownership—or, at a minimum, privatisation of management—should be specified and implemented. While it may be desirable for some industries and services (e.g. some forms of transport) to continue under government ownership and management, the entire issue should be approached pragmatically (rather than dogmatically) with maximum efficiency and profitability and potential for contribution to economic recovery and growth the prime considerations. An autonomous Eritrean administration should avoid proliferation of government bureaucracy and government-sponsored employment schemes. The less administrative interference in the economy, the more rapidly it will recover.

Economic Policies and Principles

The new Eritrean administration will be wise to give economics priority over politics, for future political arrangements are likely to be sounder if they are grounded in economic realism. No easy assumptions about the availability of foreign aid and investment are justified. Eritrea is in competition with the rest of Ethiopia, the rest of the Horn, the rest of Africa, the entire Third World, and all former and reforming communist countries for aid and investment. Governments, international lending institutions, and private investors have a broader variety of opportunities open to them than ever before, worldwide. Funds for aid and capital for investment will not be sufficient to fill all needs and opportunities. Needs are so great that many economists forecast a worldwide shortage of investment capital during the next two decades. Most aid-givers and investors base their decisions on realistic review of prospects for success of the undertakings they support, not sentiment. Eritrea has better infrastructure, more talented people, and a more favourable geographic position than many African and Third World competitors, but these advantages alone will not ensure a flow of aid and investment. Good prospects for economic and social stability, clear legal and financial provisions, and realistic policies and political predictability are more important considerations.

The openness of the economy is also a critical factor. Autarkic, i.e. closed, economic systems are unattractive to investors. Autarky is incongruous for Eritrea, for it has been a cultural and commercial crossroads since ancient times with historic links to the Mediterranean, Africa, and the Muslim world. By itself, Eritrea's varied population is too small to be significant as a market for major manufacturers or distributors. On the other hand, the 100 million people who live in the Red Sea region (Sudan, Ethiopia, Djibouti, Somalia, Yemen, Saudi Arabia) constitute a major market that will attract investors interested in manufacturing and distribution. Eritreans are already familiar with and resident in all these areas. The Gulf, Egypt, Israel, and Europe offer further economic opportunities for Eritrea. Eritrea has open economic access to the 50 million people of Ethiopia. Poverty stricken as they may be today, they represent an enormous economic potential under a popular and constructive government. Ethiopia's existing relationships to European, African, and Middle Eastern economic development and trade groupings are advantages Eritrea can ill afford to lose. The continued strength of the Ethiopian Birr and Ethiopia's high international credit ratings represent benefits which a peaceful Eritrea would be unwise to jettison. The same is true of the services provided by long-established transport and communications facilities such as Ethiopian Airlines and the Telecommunications Authority, both of which owe part of their dependable performance to Eritrean talent. These services will be far more valuable to a peaceful and economically resurgent Eritrea than they have seemed to be in the recent past.

Haste, dogma, and emotionalism in dealing with fundamental economic issues such as these can cost Eritrea dearly and adversely affect economic and social progress—and therefore political stability—for decades to come.

Eritreans Abroad

More than a million Eritreans live outside Eritrea. There are half a million in Sudan and at least half a million in the rest of Ethiopia. There are, at a minimum, tens of thousands in the Middle East, in Europe, and in America. Many are highly educated and skilled professionals who have improved their skills and extended their knowledge while living abroad. Eritreans do not easily forget their origin. Large numbers of Eritreans send money to relatives at home. Monetary contributions from Eritreans abroad have helped sustain the struggle against the Derg. The huge Eritrean diaspora can be beneficial to a peaceful Eritrea in numerous ways—or the potential it represents can be squandered and lost. How many Eritreans will return from the Middle East, Europe, and America? Until Eritrea's economic and political situation is clear, calculation will be difficult. Some returnees may be motivated by idealism to apply their energy and experience to the rejuvenation of a peaceful Eritrea. Idealism cannot be relied upon for long as a motivating factor, however. More often than not, the decision to return—and to remain—is likely to be made on the basis of professional, financial, and family considerations. And for those accustomed to life in open societies the decision to remain is likely to be heavily influenced by the degree of openness, freedom, and opportunity that will prevail in the future Eritrea.

Many Eritreans in exile have accumulated capital to invest. This can be a valuable asset for Eritrea. Even some of those who choose not to return—and those who decide to keep a foot on both sides of the water—may be prepared to invest in undertakings in Eritrea. Those who invest will expect that their investments are well used and secure. Talented and skilled returnees are likely to expect to have a voice in economic decision making and ample opportunity to apply the experience they have gained abroad.

Eritrea is not overpopulated. Once the economy becomes reinvigorated, labour shortages may develop. Returnees from Sudan can supplement both the agricultural and industrial labour force. Many will be concerned about restoration of property rights. So will many Eritreans now living and working in other regions of Ethiopia. Eritreans continue to hold important positions in the professions, in the economy, and in public service in many parts of Ethiopia. The broad spectrum of relationships between Eritreans and Ethiopia will generate both problems and opportunities for all parties concerned. If opportunities for mutually beneficial interchange and contact not only remain open but are extended, everyone will benefit.

Expanded Economic Development in Eritrea

With the restoration of peace, many sectors of the economy which have been marking time or are entirely stagnant gain new importance. The Eritrean railway has not operated since the late 1960s. The cost and gains of refurbishing it can be calculated. The construction industry will be among the first to face opportunities for expansion. There will be high demand for construction materials. The textile and leather industries appear to offer immediate opportunities for rejuvenation and expansion, and will set in motion demand for raw materials to supply their needs. Food processing of both elementary and sophisticated products is a field with almost unlimited opportunities, both to satisfy local needs and reactivate exports.

Two fields which were only beginning to be developed in the 1960s and have remained stagnant ever since offer promising possibilities for rapid expansion and good returns in foreign exchange: (1) fishing and seafood processing, and (2) tourism. Both require relatively modest investment in infrastructure to be reactivated. They are fields well suited to private initiative. Both are likely to be attractive to foreign partners. Both can generate broad employment opportunities.

Eritrea as the Hub of its Region

From the viewpoint of geography, culture, history, and experience, the most logical region for Eritreans to relate to economically is the rest of Ethiopia. Tigre, for example, is a natural reservoir of labour for Eritrea. Ethiopian regions farther to the south are a natural source of raw materials for Eritrean industries. The rest of Ethiopia constitutes a vast market into which Eritrean industry and commercial enterprises can expand. Eritrea is a natural outlet to the sea for the rest of Ethiopia. For Tigre, Gondar, and Wollo there is no practical substitute.

I have often compared Eritrea of the past two decades to Lebanon in its present deteriorated condition[2]. There are many basic similarities between the two territories, but they are not all negative; some are positive. Until a quarter century ago, Lebanon was the economic and cultural focal point of the Arab and Eastern Mediterranean world. Beirut was a financial and trading centre equalled by no other in the region. Wealth flowed in from many directions. Banks and multi-national companies maintained regional headquarters there. Students flocked to Beirut for higher education. Arabs from a dozen countries, Iranians, Armenians, Greeks, and Turks concluded business arrangements in its restaurants and night clubs and maintained summer residences in the mountains above the city.

Eritrea has many of the same characteristics and advantages in the Horn/Red Sea region that Lebanon used to have in the Levant and Arab world: It is physically attractive and its population represents a mixture of religions, cultures, languages, foreign influences and links, and different ways of life. Eritreans have commendable habits of tolerance when times are good. I have already emphasised their aptitude for enterprise and trade. A peaceful Eritrea, with an efficient administration that does not intrude into every aspect of people's lives but lets them develop their talents and skills and benefit from them has the same potential to become a focal point for its entire region that Lebanon once had—and may at some future time regain.

Politics and Economics

The Ethiopian Revolution originally offered many hopeful prospects, but dominant Derg officers, backed by radical intellectuals, decided[3] to force the country into a political and economic system already mired in stagnation. Though the Soviets pretended their system was working and, until the mid-1980s at least, kept urging the Derg to emulate it, the failures of Marxist-Leninism were already apparent in Eastern Europe and admitted in China from the late 1970s onward. The Derg was wilfully blind to Chinese economic reforms and rejected East European advice in forcing a classic communist economic and political structure on Ethiopia. Dominant elements in both the EPLF and the TPLF long shared the same Marxist myopia. They became realists sooner. Though the sincerity of the change among both EPLF and TPLF leaders is still frequently questioned and suspicion of authoritarianism still disturbs some observers[4], I find it difficult to believe that intelligent men can fail to grasp the significance of what has been happening in the world, and the implications for the people with whom they are most concerned.

A peaceful Eritrea will not remain peaceful if it becomes a police state, if leaders attempt to impose dogma on a population that is fed up with ideology. On the other hand, if economics takes priority over politics, if political decisions are made with beneficial economic impact as the priority, the energies of the population will be absorbed in useful work and planning for the future. Political, religious, and social tensions will be reduced and awkward decisions can be left for the future. The outer world will judge Eritrea primarily by (1) the success of Eritreans in avoiding exacerbation of religious, ethnic, and social antagonism, and (2) the degree of economic momentum its leaders and people are able to sustain—and will provide help and support in response to evidence that it will be effectively used. A system moving toward democracy is a necessary requirement for generating real economic momentum. A genuinely democratic Eritrea will have a positive impact on the entire region of which Eritrea forms a part—indeed, of which Eritrea is the hub.

1 E.g., *Rebels and Separatists in Ethiopia*, The RAND Corporation, R- 3347-USDP, December 1985; and *Eritrean Options and Ethiopia's Future*, The RAND Corporation, N3021-USDP, September 1989; also "Ethiopia and the Challenge of Liberation," address at the EPD symposium in Crystal City, Virginia, 10 March 1990.

2 E.g. in "The Endless War", *Washington Quarterly*, 9/2, Spring 1986, p. 34.

3 The people themselves did not "choose" Marxism-Leninism, contrary to Mengistu's oft-repeated claims. They were never given the opportunity to express themselves until the 1987 referendum on the WPE-devised constitution, when the choice was illusory, for the so called "Workers' Party" (itself illusory) had already been imposed on the country.

4 See, e.g., "An Unborn Nation" in *The Economist*, 20-26 October 1990.

7 Sudan: State Building and the Seeds of Conflict

PETER WOODWARD

It has become common to depict the problem of Sudan's civil war as being one of 'Arab Muslim North' and 'African Christian South', yet conflict in Africa is rarely as simple as the attempts to fit it into such neat categories. First, conflict arises from dynamic processes rather than simply the existence of different categories; and second, the juxtaposition of various communities, whether defined in racial, religious or regional categories, is not sufficient to account for conflict. Instead the causes of conflict may be analysed initially in terms not of the differences represented in the fighting, but the shared experience, which for many of the conflicts in Africa means being incorporated into the same state.

For its part the state in Africa has rarely been that desired Western institution: a neutral state for political direction by an elected government chosen by fair and open election by all the citizens. Rather it was, in origin, usually an alien and imposed framework which in its days of foreign rule imposed a discriminatory domination, and which in the years since independence has all too often become a source of deep rivalry between competing segments of the indigenous population, to the point at which the institutions of government were found wanting, and where the survival of the state itself sometimes has been threatened.

Issues such as Christian versus Muslim and African versus Arab are, in the context of the post-independence period, in part at least a product of the state; and in large measure a consequence of the state-building that has taken place since imperialism carved out the state boundaries of most of modern Africa.

This concentration on the state and its role in shaping the relations between various communities and identities is particularly relevant in

Sudan in view of the lack of autonomous pre-imperial progress of Arabism and Islam south of the thirteenth parallel. There was strong resistance to penetration further south, and, as has been remarked, the difficulties of integration 'have far deeper roots than the misdeeds of alien administrators...but the chapters of southern history which followed the opening up of the south after 1840 certainly helped to create these problems'[1]. These chapters not only open relatively early in African terms, but Sudan also experienced two different imperial powers, Turco-Egyptian as well as British rule, and two periods of independence when the Mahdist state from 1885-98 is recalled, as well as the period since 1956. This chapter reviews the development of the state throughout the imperial years and seeks to outline its contribution to the development of conflict between north and south in Sudan.

Founding the State : Turco-Egyptian Rule 1820-1865

Sudan's first experience of state creation within approximately its present boundaries occurred during the period of Turco-Egyptian expansion which began in 1820. That experience evolved through different stages, but has to be seen in origin as related to developments within Egypt itself. Indeed throughout much of its period of independence, as well as during the periods of direct imperial control, developments in the relations between north and south in Sudan were at least influenced, if not actually shaped, by issues and forces external to Sudan itself. Thus, in origin, the South's relations with the north derived principally from the overall experience of Turco-Egyptian penetration, which, in its turn, derived ultimately from the needs of Egypt herself as perceived by her own dynamic and ambitious leaders, especially Mohammed Ali and later the Khedive Ismail.

Mohammed Ali had a number of motives for embarking on his conquest of Sudan, including the political necessity of finally crushing Mamluk resistance, as well as his quest for land, minerals and slaves, but one recent book remarks that, in general, "expansion was economic planning carried out by other means"[2].

In the south, the coming of Turco-Egyptian penetration from 1840 did, indeed, reflect the primacy of economic influences, for trade was to precede any attempt to establish an administrative structure in the region by 20 years. Turco-Egyptian rule was by no means the start of trade and commerce in the Sudan, but there was a considerable expansion of trade, with exports initially controlled by government monopolies, though smuggling also existed. Livestock, indigo and sugar cane were exports which had some success, as well as gum arabic and ostrich feathers. It is partly within this context that the South's main contribution, ivory and slaves, must be seen. The former may appear more benign, except to conservationists, and yet it was the search for that commodity which first created major conflict in the south. Growing demand as far away as Europe and America was clamouring for ivory and this new penetration deep into Africa proved most profitable. But while the trade began peacefully enough, with indigenous inhabitants delivering tusks to the European-led traders on the upper Nile, it proved impossible to maintain a stable trading relationship and it became necessary to use increasing violence to ensure supplies, leading in time to the establishment of armed camps away from the Nile, initially primarily to continue the quest for ivory.

That form of violent extraction was bad enough, in terms of local relations, but much worse was to follow with the development of the slave trade, though here, too, it fitted the overall experience of Turco-Egyptian penetration of Sudan. The acquisition of labour for Egypt's economic development, as well as for her army, was a major motive of Mohammed Ali, and slaving had gone on extensively from the Funj in the east to the Nuba mountains in the west before the penetration deeper into the south. But, by that time Mohammed Ali's dreams had long faded and much of the slave drive fulfilled not so much the purposes of the state as of those it had encouraged to seek their fortunes in the region. Ivory merchants saw their followers, many Danaqla or Shaygiyya from the main Nile, indulge in their own private slaving, not only from financial motives but also because domestic slavery was widely accepted in northern Sudan and currently recognised in Islam. In addition, there were the professional slave traders, the big men who were a power in themselves and not only in Sudan.

In turn, these elements and the itinerant armed traders from the north, the *jallaba*, became the dominant force in much of the region, leading Richard Gray to remark "thus throughout the southern Sudan ... a new ruling caste of traders established itself during the 1860s", and a little later,"The early hopes and efforts of individual European missionaries and merchants were replaced by the power and exactions of increasing numbers of Arab settlers. The deadlock between traders and tribes was broken by a violence which cumulatively created a chaos of destruction. The search for ivory brought not legitimate commerce but robbery and in some areas the slave trade was following in its train".[3]

When, during the reigns of Mohammed Said and Ismail, there were attempts by Egypt to establish an effective administration in the south and to bow to European pressures to stop the slave trade, there was relatively little change since Turco-Egyptian officials in the region frequently augmented their own pay by indulgence in the business. Even the efforts of Baker and Gordon as governors of Equatoria had only a very limited success since so many of their agents remained involved.

Horrific though this slave trade was, and the role of the Arabs of long term damage to relations between them and the southerners, it was less an aberration, than an extended and extreme form of some other developments in Sudan. As indicated, slaving had been encouraged by the state in more central areas. So too had the use of agents recruited in the north, such as the cavalry irregulars drawn from the Shayqiyya who were often used on tax-gathering expeditions which could themselves become violent affairs. The encouragement of commerce may not have resulted in the petty slaving in which Arabs increasingly indulged in the south, but other forms of petty trade dominated by riverine Arabs did spread throughout the north; and even brought its own bondage with the extension of the *sheil* system whereby peasants became heavily indebted to local merchants/money lenders. Even the involvement of officials in slaving, which so rankled with Baker and Gordon in Equatoria, fitted the country as a whole for Turco-Egyptian officials often regarded postings to Sudan as a form of banishment, for which compensation could only be found in financial aggrandisement.

Likewise, the territorial ambition of Ismail which saw the activities of Baker and Gordon in Equatoria in the context of a bid for control right down to the Indian Ocean, reflected Mohammed Ali's aim on entering Sudan of controlling the western flank of the Red Sea, with its lucrative trade, at the same time as attacking the Wahhabis in Saudi Arabia.

While these similarities can be drawn between the experiences of Turco-Egyptian rule in both north and south, clearly the experience with regard to Islam was wholly different. The north had become Muslim before the nineteenth century, while, as indicated, Islam had not advanced south of the thirteenth parallel. Turco-Egyptian involvement in the south did involve Islam (and there were also brief attempts to establish Christian missions) but the invaders were neither proselytisers, nor did they have a political use for Islam, rather it was an economic and social phenomenon. Economically, the attitudes of Islam with regard to both heathen and slaves helped in the ideological self-justification of Arab slave raiders and jellaba, just as it also justified their commercialism whether in slavery or anything else. Resistance to the intruders was thus resistance to Islam and the practices it sanctioned as well as to its agents. But there was also a reverse for not all resisted. A number of southerners did attach themselves to the fringes of the northerner's camps and begin to adopt Islamic practices and use Arabic as their lingua franca. In this way the beginnings of what was to become the Nubi community were formed. But in the context of Turco-Egyptian penetration and eventual administration this process had no overt political role, beyond giving some credence to the idea that with time at least some areas of the south might become partially receptive to Islamic and Arabic influences which had so signally failed to make any impact before the new rulers arrived.

With regard to Islam the experience of the south was obviously very different from the north during the Turco-Egyptian period, but in many other respects it was essentially a special case, rather than a region which suffered experiences which were intended to differentiate it from other parts of the country. But the means of achieving its exploitation involved not just subordination to Turco-Egyptian invaders but to their Arab and Muslim agents and followers from the riverine north.

The Mahdist Interlude 1885-1898

As P M Holt has written, "The southern Sudan was not effectively part of the Mahdist state".[4] Yet, that in itself is indicative of much about the relationship between Sudan's first independent state and the region. Ahmed al-Mahdi was by origin a Dongolawi, and his successor the Khalifa Abdullahi from the Ta'aisha Baqqara; while the revolt itself began in Gezira Aba but developed its momentum in the western Sudan, and it was only

81

after its successes there that it won wide support in the more northern and eastern areas. Nor did the reasons for the revolt, after 60 years of generally stable, if never popular, Turco-Egyptian rule derive from the south directly. Indirectly, however, its experiences played some part, for it appears that Gordon's attempts to suppress the slave trade when governor general of Sudan may have done much to provoke hostility amongst the petty traders on Islam's southern frontier; while his departure from Sudan following the deposition of Ismail in Egypt in 1877 contributed to the weakness of purpose on the part of the Turco-Egyptian officials who confronted the revolt at its outset.

Given that the revolt started in the north and featured the success of Mohammed Ahmed's claim to be Islam's Expected One, the Mahdi, it is not surprising that the south was a neglected area, which was raided rather than ruled. The core of the state lay in the centre and north-east of the former Turco-Egyptian territory, and it had trouble with its other marches, let alone the distant south. It did not have commercial or territorial ambition of the kind which its predecessor had had, nor did its theocratic goals involve the southwards extension of Islam, as much as a northwards thrust to endeavour to purify the existing but corrupt Islamic world. There was concern in the 1890s at possible European incursions in the south, but apart from a garrison for a few years at Rejaf and occasional forays the Mahdist state was relatively unconcerned. (Indeed the Turco-Egyptian appointee Emin Pasha remained as governor in Equatoria after the fall of Khartoum, and when he had gone Selim Bey and his men retained a violent and exploitative presence, while attempting "To maintain the status they claimed as soldiers of a civilised government"[5])This relative disinterest did not, however, mean that peace reigned in the south. The local risings against the collapsing Turco-Egyptian administration and raiding from the north helped ensure that the turbulence of the previous 40 years was kept very much alive.

Anglo-Egyptian Condominium 1898-1956

In contrast, the Anglo-Egyptian condominium was interested in the south from the outset. Whereas Mohammed Ali's motives had been largely economic, the new rulers' concern was primarily political: for Britain, the instigator and leader of the re-conquest, it was essentially an important chapter in the scramble for Africa. Indeed, the re-conquest was eventually to focus on the south in the form of the Anglo-French confrontation at Fashoda in 1898. Just as regional and international political issues had been at the centre of the re-conquest and the establishment of the condominium, so they were to remain throughout the period of British rule, including vital aspects of the making of the relationship between north and south.

While Britain dominated Egypt she could temporarily forget about the international political implications of Sudan, but this changed dramatically as a result of Britain's response to Egyptian nationalism at the end of World War I which resulted in Britain's unilateral declaration of Egyptian independence in 1922 and, once more, brought international political considerations to the fore. After Egypt's independence, Britain sought to negotiate a new agreement with her over defence, which Egypt understandably tried to use as a bargaining card for greater involvement in her former territory, Sudan, out of which she felt cheated by the terms of the condominium. This dispute repeatedly torpedoed negotiations until 1936 when the threat of Italy in Cyrenaica and Abyssinia posed a sufficient threat to make negotiations succeed.

It was understandable that since British rule in Sudan was essentially a political act, and one, moreover, carried out by Christians in a largely Muslim country, the management of Islam itself was a major consideration. In the task of consolidating the new imperial state, Mahdism appeared to pose a particular challenge because of its proven capacity to generate mass opposition to alien rule. In practice, it was contained initially in spite of a number of outbursts; but later it was dramatically swung round from an anti-government to a pro-government force during World War I when the Sudan Government sought to utilise its hostility to the Caliph in Istanbul. Its leader, the Mahdi's son, Sayyid Abdal al-Rahman al-Mahdi, subsequently became the most prominent collaborator with the Sudan Government. This political management of Islam had also been exercised with respects both to the *ulemma* and to the influential *sufi* orders, most notably the Khatmiyya, which became once more, as it had been in the nineteenth century, the main rival to the Mahdists.

Political management of Islam was the only policy available in northern Sudan, but in the south it was realised that, though as in the nineteenth century government stations and *jallaba* continued to spread Islam, it might be possible to contain, and even reverse this trend. In part the reasons were ideological, and the Christian missionaries were keen to stress this feature, but there were also judged to be imperative political reasons.

Egyptian nationalism not only undermined Britain's position in Egypt; it also encouraged the threat of a similar, if much weaker, movement in Sudan which gave rise to the 1924 revolt. Militarily it was contained, but politically it encouraged ideas of encouraging native administration and parcelling out the country in such a way as to counter the "septic germs" of nationalism and the pretensions of the northern Sudanese intelligentsia, itself a product of the government's education programme.

In the south native administration, the preservation of the "social organism", was to go hand in hand with endeavouring to oppose the spread of Islam. R O Collins has brought out the importance of 1924 in this through the response of financial secretary, Sir George Schuster, who saw two opposing forces inexorably moving towards each other "one Arabic and Islamic pressing up the Nile, the other English and Christian moving forward into the centre of Africa from both East & West Africa." The government should take steps "so that whatever happens the Southerner would form a sort of 'buffer state' insuring that the influence brought to bear on the African tribes in the Southern parts of the Sudan are harmonious with British influences spreading up from Kenya and Uganda."[6] Such thinking contributed directly to the isolationist tendencies of the Southern Policy introduced in 1930, but the possible 'buffer state' was considered briefly in 1931, only to be rejected because of the criticism it would raise in the north and the strong objection that Egypt would voice - these political considerations proved paramount in what in, the long term, proved the most crucial step taken by the British in Sudan in contributing to the seeds of conflict. Though the Southern Policy encouraged the use of English to replace Arabic, and Christian mission schools, it failed to eradicate northern influences entirely and produced understandable fears amongst the already existing northern intelligentsia of a plan to attach the south to East Africa, while it deliberately sought to avoid the educational steps which might produce such an unwanted intelligentsia in the south.

Though British rule in Sudan existed more for political purposes than for direct economic exploitation of the country, some development was necessary, albeit reluctantly conceded by some officials, if only to pay for the state itself. To this end as well as the provision of cotton to Lancashire the Gezira scheme was established, but before World War II there had been no comparable development in the south which remained more generally on a "care and maintenance" footing, while tribal rejuvenation was attempted.

The Turco-Egyptian endeavour under Ismail to create a state covering the length of the Nile Valley and beyond, had been replaced by a British attempt at political re-division, but one in which Britain sought to keep a finger in each pie - Egypt (still by far the major interest), northern Sudan, and the south. Yet in retaining these institutional links - the condominium and a single Sudan - Britain was providing the mechanism for the continued interaction of the peoples of the Nile Valley in spite of policies aimed at their greater mutual isolation. It was a paradox which was to become unsustainable once Britain's political domination began seriously to weaken. That was to happen from 1935 to 1945, beginning with the fears which promoted the 1936 Anglo-Egyptian Treaty and ending with the aftermath of World War II.

The Anglo-Egyptian Treaty not only raised Egyptian interest in Sudan once more, it also marked the public re-birth of Sudanese nationalism which had been suppressed after 1924. Nationalism in the main towns of northern Sudan had no reflection in the south which lacked any significant intelligentsia, partly as a result of past educational and administrative policies. Though loyal in World War II the nationalists made strong demands in 1942, and once the conflict was over flowered into political parties with sectarian backing. This new political force had particular attitudes towards the fundamental question of the future shape of Sudan which had major repercussions for the south. Ambiguity had long existed about eventual relationships with Egypt, and the latter's interest was exploited by the Sudanese 'unionists' as they were known; while their anti-Egyptian opponents, the Mahdist-backed Umma Party, collaborated in constitutional advance with the Sudan Government on condition that the other ambiguity, the south, be resolved only on the basis of full incorporation into a unitary state. The combination of a lack of its own adequate representation and northern insistence, against the increasing fears of southerners and the advice of British officials in the region on the full incorporation of the south, meant that, effectively, from 1946 to 1956 the south was swept along by political events on which it could have little influence, but which appeared to resolve both that region's future and the independence of Sudan from Egypt.[7]

1   L M Passmore Sanderson and G N Sanderson, *Education, Religion and Politics in Southern Sudan 1899-1964*, London, 1981, p 9
2   Afaf Lufti al Sayyid Marsot, *Egypt in the reign of Mohammed Ali*, Cambridge, 1984, p197
3   Richard Gray, *A History of Southern Sudan*, London 1979, p110
4   P M Holt and M W Daly, *The History of the Sudan*, London 1979, p10
5   Lugard, quoted in Peter Woodward 'Ambiguous Amin', *African Affairs*, 77, 307, April 1978, p162
6   Quoted in R O Collins *Shadows in the Grass*, New Haven, 1983, p170
7   Peter Woodward, 'The South in Sudanese Politics', *Middle Eastern Studies*, 16, 3 October 1980

8 Conflict and Federalism in Sudan

PETER WOODWARD

The current debate about democracy in Africa focuses on moves to replace one-party and military regimes with multi-party political systems. But alongside that is a less heard but parallel discussion of the appropriate form of constitution, including that of the unitary state or the creation of forms of federalism. Neither of the debates is new: back at independence in the 1950s and '60s, hopes were attached to both forms of government, though then in combination. Now the relationship between the two is far less clear. Nigeria plans to espouse federalism, for the third time, if and when it returns to civilian rule in 1993; but 'multi-partyism' is confined to two political parties as prescribed and vetted by the retiring military president. Elsewhere, as will be seen, the debate on federalism is pursued without an apparent intention even to take on the constrained 'multi-partyism' of Nigeria, but appears to envisage federalism accommodating national diversity by allowing for regional variations rather than opening up national competition.

The essence of this approach is that the major sources of political conflict in Africa, and particularly in the Horn where federalism has been variously suggested for Ethiopia, Somalia and Sudan, lie in regional conflicts which are themselves reflections of ethnic, cultural or racial differences, or some combination of these themes. There is thus a direct link made between the numerous conflicts of the Horn and the regions in which they arise; and measures to alter the state accordingly leads to something loosely called 'federalism'. There may be ways forward towards peace by encouraging parties in conflict to think of settling their differences in this way. Governments may be persuaded to give up a degree of power to regional bodies of some kind; and regionally-based resistance movements may be persuaded to settle for half a loaf and surrender any dreams of secession. Numerous conferences by well-intentioned outsiders have been convened down the years, apparently predicated upon some such outcome. The problem, however, arises when what is seen as the problem is not simply the degree of power held centrally, and therefore the vision of power to be negotiated, but the character of the state as well.

In the case of Sudan federalism has been discussed since before independence in 1956, and as a result (as in Ethiopia) has already acquired a chequered history of its own that will be reflected in the attitudes and discussions about conflict resolution. Alongside this, and partly arising from it, are differing perceptions of the state itself. It is not simply regarded as a locus of power to be divided by agreement, but a structure of power which, in itself, contains many contradictory aspirations which could defy a simple division of political power. It is the contention of this paper that the recent struggles over federalism in Sudan reflect very different perceptions not only of that concept, but of the state itself, and that, in the struggle, federalism has evolved as much as a weapon as a solution. In consequence, there is no easy route to peace that can be centred around a direct pursuit of a 'federalist compromise' between the existing military regime and its National Islamic Front backers on the one hand, and its major challengers, the Sudan Peoples Liberation Army (SPLA), on the other. This paper will therefore trace the background to conflict from the standpoint of the nature of the state in Sudan, before moving on to look at the civil war itself, at the nature and role of the federal debate, and at the adoption - or more properly imposition - of federalism in early 1991.

State and Civil War

Although the Sudan Peoples Liberation Army (SPLA) has since 1983 been fighting a war which it sees as ending the repression of a 'ruling clique' over the whole country, it has to be remembered that in reality the war has been fought overwhelmingly in the south of the country.[1] And the reason for this is not simply that the south is 'different' from the north, especially in regarding itself predominantly as African rather than Arab and Christian rather than Muslim, but because the south has historically done badly from the state roughly as presently constituted in Sudan.

Even before the first imperial invasion into what became al-Sudan by the Turco-Egyptian forces of Mohammed Ali in 1820, the integrative influences of the Arabic language and Islam which had been penetrating northern Sudan for centuries (generally peacefully) had not reached south of the thirteenth parallel i.e. into the south. A combination of physical obstacles, especially the Sudd (the vast Upper Nile swamp), and the hostile response of Nilotic communities towards invaders kept them at bay. From about 1840 as the rapacious commercial tentacles of the new rulers in Khartoum reached down into the south, first for ivory and then for slaves, they did so by means of violence which did great damage to many indigenous communities. The Mahdist state which was established following the final defeat of the Turco-Egyptians in 1885 brought little respite. It was a northern-based regime increasingly centred around the Baqqara Arabs of western Sudan, and while making little attempt to control or administer the south it perpetuated the relationship of violence through intermittent slave-raiding.

The Anglo-Egyptian condominium, established following the Battle of Omdurman in 1898, was in reality British rule; and while the northern Sudan was treated with some care, fearing a recrudescence of Mahdism, the British, too, proved very free with violence in the south in the first 30 years of their administration. In the name of 'pacification' there were numerous 'punitive raids' to crush resistance, burn villages and confiscate cattle. A policy for administering the south only began after World War I and, by 1930, had become the notorious isolationist 'Southern Policy'. Following the 1924 revolt in Khartoum, which was seen by the British as a result of the post-war explosion of Egyptian nationalism, Sudan as a whole was to be subject to retrenchment through 'Native Administration'; which in the south meant also attempts to encourage Christianity rather than the spread of Islam and vernacular languages and English instead of Arabic, a development which was historically to be very important in subsequent emerging 'southern' consciousness.

While the south was subject to violence and then isolation, in northern Sudan there had been peace, a modest prosperity, especially with the expansion of cotton growing, and a wider and higher standard of education. All this was to make the north the main centre of Sudanese nationalism as it grew after World War II, and it demanded successfully the full incorporation of the south in the constitutional steps from 1948 to self-government in 1954 and independence in 1956. The south could only express concerned acquiescence in these developments though the dangers to come were presaged by the mutiny of army units in August 1955 and the widespread killing of northerners resident in the south.

After independence, successive northern-dominated governments, both civilian and military, were unsuccessful in handling the growing southern problem, ranging from neglect to attempts to reverse the British isolation by enforced Arabisation and Islamisation. These policies proved counterproductive, and from 1962 sustained guerrilla warfare developed which ended ten years and several regimes later, when it was in the interest of both Nimeiri's regime and the Anya-nya to negotiate peace at Addis Ababa in 1972. In retrospect, however, the decade of regional government that followed looks more like a truce than a peace, and by the early 1980s the short-term causes of the present conflict were emerging. Economic progress in the south after the agreement of 1972 had proved difficult and slow, but when at the end of the decade two major new projects started, the oil around Bentiu and the building of the Jonglei Canal, they produced real fears that Nimeiri intended to exploit them for the benefit of the north rather than the south. Meanwhile, within southern politics ethnic tensions were growing, especially between Dinka and Equatorians, giving rise to the question of re-dividing the Southern Region into three, an argument in which Nimeiri directly participated, eventually coming down for re-division. In addition, in September 1983, shortly after the SPLA had taken shape, Nimeiri suddenly introduced sharia (Islamic) laws, which were particularly repugnant to southerners and fuelled opposition to his government. Thus, by the end of 1983 the deep-seated problems of southern Sudan had been exacerbated by various actions of government which contributed to the collapse of the earlier peace and a new round of civil war.[2]

Course of the War

The war initially had a slow build-up. After the Addis Ababa agreement the decision to merge 6,000 ex-Anya-nya into the army was always difficult to implement. Tension was deep, and poor conditions in units in the south, especially with regard to pay and supplies, led to a number of local incidents. At the same time local administration in the countryside had proved hard to re-build after 1972 and there were growing reports of lawlessness, especially on the east bank of Upper Nile. A further factor threatening security was the instability and violence in neighbouring states as Ethiopia experienced turmoil in the late 1970s and early 1980s, including swathes of the country's western areas, and in Uganda the collapse of the Amin regime brought an influx of refugees, guns and money into southern Sudan.[3] This increasingly unstable security situation, coupled with perception of Khartoum's malevolence towards the south and the intra-southern political differences, contributed directly to the re-opening of civil war in 1983.

What finally tipped the scales from localised violence to a more widespread conflict was the wave of mutinies in 1983, especially the one amongst the garrison at Bor in Upper Nile. In addition to the customary grievances about pay and supplies there was great hostility at an order that the Bor garrison was to be transferred to the north. This was at best inept, and may have been deliberately provocative. The order brought back memories of a similar one which precipitated the mutiny of 1955, and as if movement to the north was not seen as sufficiently threatening in itself stories were also circulating of Sudanese troops being sent to Iraq as a contribution to the Iran-Iraq war. At the time of the mutiny an ex-Anya-nya officer who was from the Bor area originally, Lt-Colonel John Garang de Mabior, went to the garrison and finished up emerging as leader of the mutineers and leading them over the border into Ethiopia. Here, refugee camps had already developed amongst those fleeing from the growing insecurity of eastern Upper Nile, and in Ethiopia the mutineers were subsequently joined by hundreds of disaffected police, game wardens and press officers, most of whom had some experience of both firearms and discipline.

The situation in Ethiopia was especially propitious for them. The Ethiopian government had by 1983 re-captured much of the ground lost to earlier guerrilla opposition groups, most notably the Eritreans, but also others further south such as the Ethiopian Democratic Union (EDU). It was the Ethiopian perception that the survival of opposition owed much to the continuing support provided by the supply routes across Sudan from Port Sudan, as well as the activities of the insurgents in the huge refugee camps in eastern Sudan which had mushroomed with the intensification of conflict after 1977. One way of counteracting what can seem, at best, as Sudanese acquiescence in this situation was to support Sudan's opponents, especially this new group around Garang which became known as the Sudan People's Liberation Army (SPLA) and claimed, too, to be creating a broad political movement, the Sudan People's Liberation Movement (SPLM). Ethiopia herself was being assisted militarily by Cuba as well as the Soviet Union, and, in time, Cuban training was extended to the SPLA. SPLA soldiers went for courses in Addis Ababa, and some were even flown to Cuba itself for advanced instruction. At the same time Libya, which had long opposed Nimeiri's regime, entered into a closer relationship with the Marxist states of Ethiopia and South Yemen. Libya, with her vast, then largely unused, stocks of Soviet arms became the main supplier of weapons to the SPLA in an attempt to precipitate Nimeiri's downfall. In an age of the new Cold War with a hawkish United States, and the Soviet Union ever more committed in Afghanistan, it was easy to see a picture of superpower confrontation developing with Egypt and Sudan, backed by the United States, countering the Aden Treaty. But this was a simplification which saw the guerrilla movements, including the SPLA, as proxies and pawns on a global map, rather than as movements rooted in real and particular disputes in the various countries.

Ideologically, the SPLA/SPLM was from the outset radical rather than Marxist, and considerably more sophisticated than the old Anya-nya had been. Although based in the south, it was not secessionist but stood instead for a 'new Sudan' in which there could be federalism or regionalism, just as long as central domination by a 'ruling clique' was prevented. It did not specifically seek a one-party state, but spoke of democracy in a way which made clear its criticism of Sudan's old parties while seeking to give power to the masses. Socially, it sought to end what was seen as past Arab racism and to promote social and economic justice by reversing the uneven development which it claimed Sudan had experienced hitherto. On religion it sought secularism, and this received a great enhancement with Nimeiri's declaration of *sharia* (Islamic law) in September 1983.

All this, however, was somewhat academic in 1983 when the SPLA first began to take to the field. The core of the SPLA has been Dinka, the largest ethnic grouping in the south, and it was natural that the first areas in which it operated were the Dinka territories in Upper Nile and Bahr al-Ghazal. But in travelling to and from their Ethiopian bases the Dinka SPLA frequently confronted their traditional rivals the Nuer. Among the Nuer there had already been a number of guerrilla groups loosely known as Anya-nya 2, and rivalry between it and the SPLA led to fierce clashes between the two forces. By the end of 1984 Anya-nya 2 had suffered setbacks, and it decided to become one of the early militias armed by the government: but in spite of this new source of weapons the SPLA continued to make headway. As well as inflicting damage on Anya-nya 2 the SPLA took a number of small garrisons, and had already stopped work on the two major projects - the oil field around Bentiu and the Jonglei Canal. As the SPLA grip on the region strengthened so more and more of the Nuer went over to it, and in late 1987 the bulk of Anya-nya 2 defected to the SPLA leaving only a few clans and some older Nuer to continue collaboration with the government, loosely in and around the one main remaining stronghold, the regional capital of Malakal.

The greatest concentration of Dinka is in Bahr al-Ghazal, and here the SPLA had rapid successes in the countryside. To counter it the army once again turned to militias, especially from the Rizeigat and Misiriya sections of the Baqqara Arabs of Southern Kordofan known as *murahaleen*.[4] The Baqqara have historically had uneasy relations with the Dinka to the south, though with negotiation there have been periods of peace. In the 1980s however circumstances combined here as well to encourage violence. The drought in western Sudan in 1984-85 brought southern pressures in Kordofan as tribes moved from the arid north in search of pastures. At the same time the herds were hit, and young men in particular saw an opportunity to raid the Dinka cattle which had been less damaged. There were even traders willing to invest in raiding (summoning images of the nineteenth century - and there was apparently slaving as well), since meat supplies to central Sudan from the west had been curtailed by the drought. As well as local tribesmen, southern Kordofan also saw the return in the early 1980s of *ansar*, the followers of the Mahdi family who had been trained in Ethiopia and Libya to fight against Nimeiri with whom Sadiq al-Mahdi had made an uneasy peace in 1977. After he came to power in 1986 Sadiq was keen to encourage the *ansar* to become a recognised para-military force and they too were used with the *murahaleen*. The American oil company, Chevron, also wished to see the oil fields at Bentiu re-captured, not least because it feared a loss of the concession (its largest in Africa) if it was not seen by Sadiq alMahdi's government to be joining the efforts against the SPLA and in 1987 was alleged to have backed Misiriya *murahaleen*. Lastly, and most importantly, the army welcomed the experience and mobility of the *murahaleen* and was happy to arm and encourage them in raids that seemed like a scorched earth policy in northern Bahr al-Ghazal. Many people, particularly the older men, women and children left behind by young Dinka warriors joining SPLA, were forced to move north for aid in refugee camps around towns such as Abyei and accounted for many of the hundreds of thousands estimated to have died from famine and related disease in the conflict.

Further south in Bahr al-Ghazal, in and around the regional capital of Wau, there were clashes between the SPLA and other smaller groups known as the *fertit* who always feared Dinka domination. The *fertit* were encouraged by the army to form their own militia, and in 1987 there was fighting and massacres in Wau itself, in which many civilians died.

In Equatoria the position was even more confused. The smaller, more settled communities of Equatoria have long had mixed feelings about the Nilotic pastoralists from the two neighbouring regions. These tensions had emerged in southern politics in the 1970s and the Equatorians were the main proponents of re-division to escape what they saw as Dinka domination. Equatoria was also the area most affected by the anarchy of northern Uganda, and there has often been cross border movement involving Kenya as well as various armed groups. In late 1985 and 1986 the SPLA started to push down into Equatoria in force, in the face of which the army gave weapons to a number of tribal militias such as the Latuka and Toposa, with the latter using them to raid into Kenya as well leading Kenya effectively to occupy the Ilemi triangle and become more pro-SPLA. However, the SPLA was only briefly checked by the militias and continued in control of most of eastern Equatoria, finally by early 1989 surrounding the regional capital of Juba itself, which was then supplied only by air. The SPLA pressed on into western Equatoria as well, though the Azande country, always something of an anomaly in southern politics, proved more difficult to penetrate.[5]

Overall much of the south has been captured by the SPLA, and the government controls little apart from some larger towns, including Malakal, Juba and Wau, which it continues to supply only with difficulty. Neither the army nor the southern militias have proved effective in stopping the SPLA, which has also carried the war north into Blue Nile Region, capturing the border town of Kurmuk twice, as well as threatening Kadugli in southern Kordofan. The war has been far more widespread than the earlier conflict, reaching into most areas of the south, but it has often taken the form of local wars in which local issues were involved rather than being simply a war of two armies with national objectives. For some, such as the *murahaleen*, the war has become virtually a business. The scale and intensity of the war has led to an estimated half a million deaths in a population put in 1983 at a little over five million. In addition perhaps two million have been displaced, mainly to northern Sudan, especially the slums around Khartoum, or to the camps in Ethiopia. The human cost has thus been appalling as, too, has the damage caused to the infrastructure in the south itself; while the war has cost a huge amount to the already bankrupt and indebted government in Khartoum.[6] It was partly due to this realisation of the damage on the part of the United Nations, and partly that with SPLA successes the war had reached something of a military pause, that in 1989 both sides agreed a temporary cease-fire while supplies for the civilian population known as Operation Lifeline - were rushed in. However, by the end of that year, the cease-fire had broken down and there was renewed fighting in several areas. In Juba itself the SPLA was calling on civilians to leave and outside agencies were evacuating most expatriates as the conflict escalated. In 1991 the SPLA itself split into two major factions and intra south fighting developed, further complicating the overall picture of conflict.

Impact of the War

The war followed its own logic of escalating violence and destruction from 1983 to early 1989, in spite of the changing political situation in Khartoum. On these it most certainly had an influence, but it was one amongst a number of essentially conflicting political and economic factors all of which were contributing to a steady deterioration in Sudan on all fronts.

Nimeiri's reckless meddling in southern politics, which had done so much to lose him support in a region in which he had once been acclaimed a hero (more so than he ever was in the north), was partly due to the fact that like successive northern governments his first concern at a time of increasing difficulty was with Khartoum politics. Once he took the SPLA seriously and realised that he would get no direct external involvement to bolster his beleaguered army, he panicked into offering Garang virtual overlordship of the south in return for peace, but it was never likely to attract his radical and idealistic young opponent. The SPLA liked to think its military successes contributed to the *intifada* (uprising) of April 1985 that overthrew Nimeiri, and so it did but essentially indirectly. The intelligentsia, directly in the line of the radical nationalist strand which ran from the early Graduates Congress through the leadership of October revolution of 1964 that overthrew Abboud's regime, had become increasingly restive and professional unions had staged a number of damaging strikes in the early '80s. They certainly felt sympathetic to many of the criticisms expressed by the SPLA, but they were far from being the Khartoum branch of the SPLM.[7] It was the growing isolation of Nimeiri, together with the preceding riots showing economic discontent, as well as knowledge of the military successes of the SPLA, that led the intelligentsia, under the banner of the National Alliance for National Salvation (NANS), to take to the streets in the face of the security forces who appeared to capitulate before them, abandoning Nimeiri to exile and forming the Transitional Military Council (TMC) to work with a civilian cabinet of non-politicians.

At this moment there probably was an important difference of perception. For the Alliance the *intifada* had been a heroic achievement, and the TMC formula was a way of throwing out Nimeiri without a violent confrontation on the streets of the capital. The TMC was only an interim move and during its one year duration Sudan would move to end the war and establish a new constitution. However, from the fighting front in southern Sudan the situation looked very different to the SPLA. Nimeiri had gone, but the TMC was a sleight of hand, and the essence of his regime still remained in the form of the leaders of the army they were fighting against, now reconstituted as the TMC. The masses had risen, but the Alliance had at least miscalculated and at worst 'Intellectuals and top bureaucrats who predominate, across the entire Sudanese political spectrum, have their distinct socio-class interests to defend'.[8]

The SPLA's position on negotiations will be seen shortly, but what is of importance here is that the failure of the TMC and the SPLA to come together, and the former's preference to hand the whole thing over to its elected civilian successors, working for want of anything else under the old Westminster-style constitution, ensured that the elections in 1986 were not able to be conducted in large areas of the south. In consequence, not only was the SPLA not represented in the new National Assembly, continuing instead with the war, but the southern politicians who were elected had varying attitudes to the SPLA and the war, as well as being open to the blandishments of the larger, richer, better-organised major parties as they competed to form successive weak coalition governments.

Once more, the influence of the war on politics was significant but indirect. Central to many of the manoeuvres in relation to the successive coalition governments that Sadiq al-Mahdi put together between May 1986 and the end of June 1989 was the question of *sharia*; and behind the question of *sharia* lay the importance of agreement with the SPLA. It was the smallest of the three main parties, the National Islamic Front (NIF), backed by the Muslim Brotherhood, which was most rigidly committed to *sharia*, for to surrender that for an ideological party of its character was to surrender its *raison d'être*. Sadiq, as leader of the Umma Party, seemed tied in principle but prepared at various times to consider amendment of existing laws rather than repeal. But it was the Unionists, initially reluctant to join the meetings with the SPLA, who finally went to the clearest commitment in November 1988 making an agreement with the SPLA by which both agreed on the freezing of the *sharia* criminal code pending the proposed constitutional conference. It led initially to the Unionists' exodus from the coalition, until rising pressure for peace early in 1989 forced Sadiq's ejection of the NIF instead and the return of the Unionists to government. It was widely rumoured shortly before the coup of 30 June 1989 that Sadiq too was being forced to the position of the Unionist-SPLA agreement, with the implication that this caused the coup by officers opposed to it.

With the political situation in Khartoum having changed so dramatically since the outbreak of the war in 1983, it is the SPLA which has been more coherent and more continuous in its position with regard to peace. In broad terms the principles it enunciated from an early stage remain central to its position at the start of 1990, but its attitude to the peace process and position in direct negotiation with successive governments in Khartoum have altered, partly as a result of the SPLA's reading of the fast changing scene.

In many ways it is clearer what the SPLA dislikes in the past, than what it actually wants to see in the future, though to be fair it has consistently said that the nature of the final outcome is a matter for a constitutional conference at which all major groups in Sudan are represented .

A notable difference between the SPLA and the Anya-nya of the earlier war is that the former declares itself unambiguously for a united Sudan, and does not favour secession in any shape or form. While this has been the consistent and unquestioned position of SPLA leaders, it also appears possible that at lower levels of the organisation the commitment may be as much to a region or even an ethnic community as to a united Sudan and, thus, there is perhaps greater potential for secessionist sentiment than emerges in official statements and positions.

The best known aspect of the SPLA's position is its hostility to *sharia* and its determination to pursue instead a secular Sudan, a position it has maintained from the outset of the conflict. While described as the 'Religious Question' it would be wrong to see it in simply religious terms. For the SPLA it is a question less of faith than domination, and thus a part of the old Sudan to be thrown off and replaced by the 'New Sudan' of which it speaks regularly. It reflects, the SPLA believes, the identity projected by Sudan's past 'ruling clique', and sharia is one aspect of 'the image of an exclusively Arab and Islamic Sudan'[9]. Just as central to SPLA's pronouncements in the past, and much more ambiguous, is the concept of 'nationality'. The SPLA is very attached to this term while being ultimately unclear to what it is actually referring.

According to the SPLA 'the ruling class is drawn from one nationality, that is the Arabicised Sudanese who also profess Islam'. In reality the SPLA argues that Sudan is compound of a number of nationalities, implying more than simply 'north' and 'south' and it seeks a 'New Sudan' in which 'members of the different Sudanese Nationalities enjoy opportunities of taking part in the decision-making process in Khartoum at all levels.'[10] It is not clear what the SPLA considers a 'nationality' to be. At times it seems to be speaking of ethnic communities, but this is both complex and confusing. It suggests a return to an old anthropological dream of an ethnographic map of Sudan. But deciding, let alone utilising, ethnic identity is not simple, and, indeed, 'ethnicity' owes as much to national politics as to primordial identity. There are, too, great problems of social mixing, such as the presence of many southerners in the north which raises the problem of the significance of 'national' identity in any form of geographical representation? Somewhat more confusing is the hope that 'the different' nationalities making up Sudan can, and will have to, coalesce into a Sudan Nation (National Formation) with its own distinct civilisation[11] The whole issue of what the SPLA calls the 'Nationality Question' is thus fraught with problems if it is pursued as a specific theme in any constitutional conference.

While the details of a future constitution should be left to a future conference to decide, it is clear that the SPLA has long wanted effective devolution to 'authentic autonomous regional governments',[12] which again means something better than past efforts. This may well be on a federal basis, which has been discussed since the preparation for independence in late 1955, 'The crux of the matter is not whether our country ought to be administered within a centralised or decentralised government but rather who should be charged with the responsibility of operating the Central government among whose key duties is the transfer of a measure of its authority to the regions'.[13]

One of the charges against the past 'ruling circles' is that they contributed to and benefited from Sudan's 'peripheral subservient role in economic development'.[14] This economic exploitation has to be stopped and replaced by a more equitable programme of economic development which will maximise what the SPLA's believes to be the country's significant resources for the benefit of all its peoples. Ideally this would be in the context of moves towards 'a New International Economic Order'. In addition to thorough economic reform the 'New Sudan' would require a new army in which the leaders in particular were drawn not from the 'ruling minority clique', but built as a 'synthesis of the warring parties'.[15] Emphasis is also placed on Sudan's pursuit of a non-aligned foreign policy, which presumably refers not only to western powers, but also to Sudan's future role in Middle East politics.

While views of the kind mentioned above have been expressed repeatedly since at least 1985, the SPLA's position in negotiations has been both limited and increasingly flexible, consistent with its view that the final outcome should lie with a national constitutional conference. Following the breakdown of talks in August 1989, John Garang reiterated four points which he believed should be the agenda for further negotiations: 'an interim broad-based government of national unity; a non-sectarian national army from both the SPLA and the regular army; a national constitutional conference; preparation for free elections'.[16] The SPLA has shown itself willing at least to talk to successive governments in Khartoum (as Garang remarked after the coup of 30 June 1989: 'We cannot shut our eyes to reality'[17]) but it would have been unreasonable not to believe that its own approach and successive talks were coloured in some way by its assessment of the bewildering changes under way in Khartoum.

It has been these changes which, on the surface at least, appear to account for so much of the failure to make peace. From the time when Nimeiri realised that the SPLA was a serious opposition and that he would have no effective support from outside Sudan to crush the movement, successive governments have adopted different positions, but always with one eye on the SPLA and the other on rivals in Khartoum. As mentioned, Nimeiri, worried at the fast deteriorating situation in the north as much as the resurgence of warfare is believed to have offered Garang virtual carte blanche in the south if he would end the conflict, but the latter was pursuing a united revolutionary Sudan and rejected it out of hand. Following Nimeiri's downfall the Transitional Military Council (TMC) was slow to move to talks, preferring to prepare the way for a return to civilian rule and let elected rulers (at least in the north) deal with the problem through a constitutional conference. Meanwhile, the SPLA pinned its hopes on the National Alliance in which the professional unions were strong and which had played a leading part in the *intifada* (uprising) that had brought Nimeiri down. These contacts, mainly in Ethiopia, led to the Koka Dam Declaration of March 1986. There was an eight point declaration at the centre of which was a call for a 'New Sudan that would be free from racism, tribalism, sectarianism and all causes of discrimination and disparity'.[18] After this came the immediate steps to be taken, including the repeal of the 'September 1983 Laws' as Nimeiri's *sharia* was called. It was then intended to proceed to a constitutional conference, provisionally to be in Khartoum in June 1986, and an agenda was agreed, on which the first two items were 'a. The Nationalities question. b. The Religious Question'. The SPLA also proposed in the Declaration that as 'an essential prerequisite' for the conference there should be a 'New Interim government of National Unity representing all the political forces including the SPLA/SPLM and the Armed Forces', though the Alliance demurred from this professing to see progress towards an elected government as planned with the TMC and the northern parties. A number of parties, including the Umma Party, endorsed the Koka Dam Declaration, but the Democratic Unionist Party (DUP) and the National Islamic Front (NIF) denounced it, especially the apparent repeal of *sharia*.

Following the election and the return of Sadiq al-Mahdi, leader of the Umma Party, as prime minister heading a coalition government, it was incumbent on him to pursue the Koka dam initiative. He met John Garang at Koka dam, where both men were suspicious of each other. In spite of this, there was some agreement, but on vital points they differed. Garang wanted the state of emergency lifted immediately since it implied that the SPLA was not a legitimate movement; and, more importantly, instead of the repeal of *sharia*, Sadiq sought amendment to the laws to make them acceptable to both Muslims and non-Muslims - the position of the coalition government.

After that failure Sadiq appeared to believe that, instead of dealing with the SPLA, he could put on new pressures. He seemed to feel that the SPLA's success owed much to the support it had received from Libya and Ethiopia, and that diplomacy, not only directly but with their major arms supplier, the USSR, would produce results. Libya had supplied the SPLA largely to bring down Nimeiri, and Sadiq al-Mahdi was an old friend of Qaddafi so it was easy to persuade him to drop his backing for John Garang. Ethiopia, however, was a tougher proposition for President Mengistu was sceptical about Khartoum and any willingness it might profess to offer the desired quid pro quo of curtailing the freedom of the Eritreans and Tigreans. In any case, while the Ethiopians had been a great help to the SPLA, with the passage of time it proved more and more capable on its own account. Sadiq had hoped that with Nimeiri gone, and his own pressure on Libya and Ethiopia, the Sudan army and the militias would be able to inflict real damage on the SPLA, but on the contrary it was overall the SPLA which continued to gain the upper hand in the south, as well as threatening in border areas as well. As a result of this unsuccessful diplomatic and military strategy it was not until the autumn of 1987 that any serious new effort was made. This time it involved a number of non-SPLA southern political groups now united as the Sudan African Parties (SAP) encouraged by the governments of Ethiopia, Kenya and Uganda, for whom the escalation of fighting into Equatoria was causing worsening problems. But, although there was some agreement upon SAP's return to Khartoum, it could make little headway with the major northern parties, that were in any case moving towards an NIF-inspired counter to the Koka Dam Declaration, the Sudan Charter (including the phrase that Muslims, 'As a matter of faith ....do not espouse secularism').

Preoccupied by the continuing instability in Khartoum there was no major new initiative until November 1988, when the DUP met with the SPLA in Addis Ababa and agreed new steps towards a constitutional conference. In particular, the SPLA conceded that, in spite of its continued wish to have *sharia* repealed, it would accept that the laws involving *hodoud* punishments, which were particularly objectionable, should be frozen in order to speed moves towards the conference. The agreement was widely welcomed in war-weary Khartoum but plunged the coalition government of DUP, Umma and NIF into crisis. Initially, Sadiq rejected the DUP initiative and the latter party left the coalition, only for popular pressure to force him to re-consider, and after protracted manoeuvring it was the NIF which had to leave with the DUP returning once more. With Sadiq still appearing slow to move it was then that the army presented a memorandum in February 1989 calling for faster progress towards peace. The situation still appeared to be confused and cynics felt Sadiq al-Mahdi remained reluctant to pursue peace, but others believed that the domestic and international pressure on him was propelling him in that direction in spite of his own feelings. However, whatever the truth, the coup led by Omar Hasan Ahmed al-Beshir on 30 June 1989, put an end to the hopes raised by the DUP in November 1988.

For those doubtful of the prospects of peace in the confusion of party politics the coup appeared at first as if it might simplify matters. The army was thought to be keen on peace, while the idea of the leaders of the two armies dealing with each other brought memories of Nimeiri's success with the Addis Ababa agreement of 1972. However, it was soon seen to be more complicated than that. The coup had been the work of middle rank officers, and there were soon widescale retirements of senior figures, indicating that the army was a less than united institution. At the same time there was soon talk of the influence of the NIF on the coup-makers, and increasingly on the government as a whole. There were contacts with the SPLA, but the first direct talks, in Nairobi in August 1989, quickly foundered on the question of *sharia* encouraging speculation of NIF influence.

The new rulers took the position that theirs was a fresh start. The old party system had been corrupt, and instead of building on past dealings with the SPLA, such as the DUP agreement of the previous year, they would make a new beginning. With many of the old party leaders in detention around one hundred prominent figures in Sudanese life were brought together in a 'National Dialogue Conference' to take the first step towards a full constitutional conference. The SPLA was invited to participate, but declined on the grounds that it had had no part in establishing the conference, which was in any case unrepresentative with many party and trade union leaders in detention.

The main recommendation of the National Dialogue Conference was that Sudan should become a nine state federation. This, it was implied, would deal with the 'nationalities question', referred to in the report as the necessity to recognise Sudan's cultural diversity, as well as with regional economic differences. Federalism was also seen as the answer to the 'religious question' for while 'Sharia and Custom shall be the two main sources of legislation in the Sudan', individual states would have the right to exempt themselves from 'legislative provisions of a purely religious character'.[19]

Armed with these recommendations the new rulers were prepared to respond to the call of former U.S. President Jimmy Carter for talks in Nairobi in December 1989. Carter saw this as part of his peace efforts for the Horn of Africa as a whole, and he appeared to have made some preliminary progress in Atlanta with the Ethiopians and the Eritreans. But the Sudan talks soon broke down once more over *sharia*, and with Carter lamenting the unwillingness of the government side, in particular, to negotiate seriously. The SPLA had expected negotiation on the four points set by Garang after the August meeting mentioned earlier, but the government sought to start instead from the National Dialogue Conference. In addition, the government rejected the old SPLA call for a new national interim government pending a constitutional conference, or that such a conference be attended by representatives of all major parties and unions.[20] As a background the new government also seemed ready to press ahead with the implementation of *sharia* which, though still on the statute book, had been effectively in abeyance ever since the fall of Nimeiri in 1985.

Following the collapse of the Carter initiative in late 1989 the regime in Khartoum has pushed ahead with its twin and related themes of federalism and the imposition of *sharia*, both effectively implementing the somewhat sketchy work of the National Dialogue Conference. In February the Fourth Constitutional Decree for 1991 announced that, as expected, there would be a nine state federation for Sudan; and the structure was as predictable as the announcement. In the north the six states are to be Khartoum, Central, Northern, Eastern, Kordofan, and Darfur; and in the south Bahr al-Ghazal, Equatoria and Upper Nile. The state governments were made responsible for administration, economic planning and development; and were to control 'trade, agriculture, forestry, environment protection, health, education, roads and transport, animal resources, water resources, tourism and housing. The state governments also have joint responsibility with the centre for urban planning, land distribution, cultural and media planning, environmental protection policies, border trade, the conduct of national censuses and supervision of the civil service.'

The decree reserved certain areas as the exclusive jurisdiction of the federal authorities. These included 'federal legislation, the affairs of the regular forces, federal defence and security matters, the judiciary, the Attorney General, the legal profession, external affairs, federal transport, higher education, currency, emergency regulations, nationality and immigration, customs, federal taxes, natural and mineral resources, federal electricity and water grid, waterways, the Auditor General's functions, federal elections and borders'.[21]

Plenty of room there for potential conflict with some important issues, such as the environment, apparently the responsibility of the individual states and the joint state-federal arrangements. Yet, in reality, there was much continuity when all the nine existing regional governors were re-appointed as governors of the new states. Nor was there much danger of their being overthrown as a result of equating federalism with multi-party democracy, calls for which the regime consistently rejected.

The second of the twin tracks, *sharia*, provided the basis for a new penal code introduced on 22 March 1991. This was 'federal legislation' since it stated explicitly that *sharia* would apply in the northern states, while in the south it would be for eventual elected assemblies to decide on the codes for each state.

Predictably, this approach to federalism, and the imposition of *sharia*, apparently to all inhabitants of northern states, whether Muslim or not, was anathema to the SPLA. Its own approach to federalism has already been seen, and the new version was regarded as a central government diktat. Rejecting the authority of the National Dialogue Conference, the SPLA also believed that the content of the proffered federation would, in reality, be one-party dictatorship by the National Islamic Front. Under the new federation 'the promotion of Arabism in these northern states will be more forceful and brutal than at any time before'.[22] And the apparent absence of *sharia* from the southern states is really no escape. Analysing the personnel announced for senior positions in the south the SPLA concluded that real power in each of the three states is in the hands of Muslims who are members or affiliates of the NIF....in all the three southern states the deputy governor is a Muslim ....all the money and economic activities of the state are put under the deputy governor ....[who] is also the minister of finance, commerce, supply and co-operatives. This put the whole state economy firmly under the NIF. They will give loans, trade, licences, etc. to members and all those sympathetic to the NIF in the southern states and deny the same to non-NIF citizens ... In all the three southern states [education and culture policy] is put under a Muslim ... this is the power of mind control ... to promote Arabism and Islamic policies in the south.

However, with continuing conflict and widespread suffering in the south attracting international concern (though not to the point of the intervention that occurred in Somalia) pressure came on both government and the SPLA to make fresh attempts at peace. The pressure was also heightened when, after the collapse of the Mengistu regime in Ethiopia in 1991 that had supported the SPLA, the movement began to fragment and even degenerate into factional and ethnic infighting. Officially a major difference within the SPLA concerned not federation, but separation of the south from the north. A number of African states, most prominently Nigeria, endeavoured to mediate between the government and the SPLA's factions. It led to talks in Abuja, Nigeria, first in June 1992 and then in May 1993, but the outcome was inconclusive.

By the second talks, between the Garang wing of the SPLA and the government, it was clear that officially it was questions of the character of a future federation that lay at the core of the disagreement. After flirting with confederation the SPLA was prepared to accept a regional federation of north and south, but thought that the secularism rather than *sharia* applied in the south, should also operate in the national capital, a condition that was unacceptable to the government side.

Conclusion

Sudan's wariness with regard to the present enthusiasm sweeping Africa for multi-party democracy is understandable. Under a simple Westminster style system it has tried that equation three times in the past, and three times it has failed. The call for federalism first emerged in the south after independence as an alternative to the unitary constitution rather than from opposition to liberal-democracy, but now the major parties to the present conflict, the government and the SPLA, appear to have thrown the baby out with the bath water. Concerned over past democratic experience they have turned to the question of federalism with different perspectives. The SPLA is openly suspicious of seeing in the government's federal formula, a move not to redress national imbalance but to perpetuate it by creating structures which will only appear to recognise regional diversity while maintaining the existing inequalities of national life. Hence the SPLA's call to tackle the problems of central government, and only then introduce measures of a possibly federal character for the regions.

In contrast, the government appears to have been keen to espouse federalism as the solution to existing regional inequalities, while also legislating for the imposition of the most contentious piece of legislation, *sharia*, throughout the north. This combination fuels the SPLA claim that it is the government in the north that risked dividing the country, and not the rebel army fighting in the south.

In spite of the obvious differences of 'north' and 'south' in Sudan, there are also major connections tending towards federalism or confederation rather than total independence. Socially, the country is far from consisting of two homogeneous blocs, but it is a much more complicated concoction, as the outbreak of intra-SPLA fighting in the south has indicated. At the same time Sudan's limited resources - oil, the Niles, and fertile land - lie at the centre of the country, and division would be complicated in theory and in practice. With the repeated failure of unitary government and the problems of separation, federalism, for all its inherent complexities, is likely to remain on the agenda for peace.

1   SPLM/SPLA Department of Information 'On the New Sudan' in A Ahmed and G Sorbo (eds), *Management of the crisis in the Sudan* (Centre for Development Studies, Bergen, 1989) p.83.

2   Important works include: P Bechtold *Politics in Sudan*, (Praeger, N.Y., 1976); Mohamed Omar Beshir, *The Southern Sudan: background to conflict* and *The Southern Sudan: from conflict to peace* (Hurst, London, 1968 and 1975); R O Collins, *Shadows in the grass* (York UP, New Haven, 1983); M W Daly *Empire on the Nile: the Anglo-Egyptian Sudan. 1898-1934* (Cambridge UP, Cambridge, 1985); T Niblock, *Class and Power in Sudan, 1898- 1985* (Macmillan, London, 1987); P Woodward *Sudan 1898-1989: the unstable state*, (Lynn Rienner, Boulder, 1990).

3   P Woodward, 'Uganda and southern Sudan: peripheral politics and neighbour relations' in H Bernt Hansen and M Twaddle (eds) *Uganda Now*, (James Currey, London, 1988).

4   Alex de Waal, 'Armed militias in contemporary Sudan', unpublished conference paper Middle East Centre/IREMAM, Oxford, December 1989. See also Amnesty International, *Sudan: human rights violations in the context of civil war*, London, December, 1989.

5   The Azande Kingdom was established in what is now Western Equatoria by incomers from the south-west and has always been a somewhat separate community aloof from the broad streams of southern politics.

6   *War Wounds: development costs of conflict in southern Sudan*, (Panos Institute, London, 1988).

7   Opponents of the National Alliance for National Salvation, particularly in the old parties and the new military regime have sought to label NANS activists as a '5th Column' of the SPLA.

8   Management of the crisis, p.90.

9   Ibid, p.83.

10   Ibid, p.85.

11   loc. cit.

12   loc. cit.

13   Ibid, p.86.

14   Ibid, p.87.

15   Ibid, p.88.

16   Sudan Update (London) 11 Aug. 1989.

17   loc. cit.

18   'Koka Dam Declaration' in *Management of the crisis*, pp.130-132.

19 *'The Steering Committee for the National Dialogue on Peace Issues, Final Report and Recommendations'*, Ministry of Foreign Affairs, Khartoum, 26 October 1989, pp.34-35.

20 Summary of World Broadcasts ME/0640 15 Dec. 1989.

21 Sudan Update, 2, 17, 20 Feb. 1991.

22 Ibid.

9 Towards an Understanding of the Somali Factor

RICHARD GREENFIELD

In understanding contemporary political attitudes either in Ethiopia or in the Somali Republic - it is imperative to recognise the importance of historical consciousness. The Ethiopian empire - which still exists in territorial extent if not in name - has often been referred to as a 'museum of cultures'.[1] Many national and linguistic groups are included within its present boundaries. These date back, in the main, only to the end of the last century - the period of the 'Scramble for Africa'. However, the imperial ambitions of the highland Amhara people to the west of the rift valley are of much longer standing. So, too, is resistance to them. The Amhara and the lowland Somalis are thus traditional enemies.

The creation of peace between them, it must be anticipated, will be difficult - as both the UN and the OAU have learned. A mural at a Somali Government exhibition on the 1982 incursion by Ethiopian troops bears out this point. A 16th-century leader, the Imam Ahmaed Ibn Ibrahim El-Ghazi (nicknamed 'Gurey', the 'left-handed') and an early 20th-century patriot, Sayyid Muhammad Abdille Hassan are portrayed handing on their weapons, typifying the national struggle, to a tank commander in the modern army. In the background a woman holds high the torch of Somali liberty. Clearly, aspects of the complicated history of the region must be surveyed in order to comprehend the tensions of today.

Ethiopian-Somali Relations: the Background

Since 'medieval' times at least, the Somalis have demonstrated - despite clan differences - considerable cultural and religious homogeneity, expressed

103

particularly when faced by external aggression. In particular this homogeneity has often been harnessed to fight off attacks of varying nature and intensity launched from the Ethiopian highlands. On the other hand, as with all nations, during periods of stress, natural cleavages widen - a tendency not one iota inhibited by irresponsible and cynical reactions on the part of political leaders, whether domestic or foreign. This has always been so.

In the 14th and 15th centuries the rulers of Abyssinia, the traditional homeland of the Amhara, the ruling Ethiopian nationality, and the Christian 'core' of the modern Ethiopian empire-state, seem to have been especially concerned to try to achieve access to the sea and to proselytise lands where Islam flourished particularly in what is now the northern part of Somalia. They sought to control trade routes which led from sea ports, such as Zeila, through the important trading city of Harar and on into the Oromo and Sidama states of the highlands. All this differed little from Crusades and Jehads elsewhere. Military expeditions were dispatched south-eastward to effect these ambitions. Resistance to them has long been a significant unifying force among Somalis and other largely Muslim nationalities .

In the 16th century the number and size of Abyssinian raiding parties, and consequent plunder and destruction, was on the increase. Eventually, the harassed Somali people retaliated. Somali armies, led by their hero - 'Gurey' - swept back across the rift valley right up into the Abyssinian highlands. His exploits and those of his forces, drawn in particular from the Darod, Isaq and Dir Somali clan-groups but also including non-Somalis, were recorded at the time and have lived on in the traditions of Abyssinians and Somalis alike. To the Somalis, his name ranks with those of later nationalists such as the Sayyid (known in late 19th and early 20th century Europe as the 'Mad Mullah') and has become an inspiration to the nationalists of today just as, in Ethiopia, it is still used to intimidate unruly or disobedient children[2] .

Such early conflicts were in a sense very straightforward - military force met military force and *de facto* and *de jure* control of territory were one and the same thing. Tribute was demanded and often paid, sometimes in more than one direction. The European 'Scramble' for African colonies in the last quarter of the 19th century - which coincided with a new expansionist phase in Ethiopian history in the reign of Menelik II - introduced a new factor which has complicated Ethiopian-Somali relations generally. In particular it lies behind the one specific problem - conflict over the Ogaden, a vast semi-desert scrub land, central to the pastoral economy of the Somalis - which developed soon after the arrival of Italian, British, French and even Russian imperial agents.

By the 1880s treaties, agreements and protectorates established by European companies and powers with Somali chieftains and dignitaries on or near the northern and eastern coasts had begun to affect the lives of people further inland. Indeed, the Ogaden Somalis soon found themselves encircled. The formula which the treaties followed with only minor variations, clearly set out as paramount the maintenance of the independence of the Somalis. Being in the main transhumantic and dependent upon herds of cattle and camels, their forefathers had, over the centuries, built up a measure of mastery over the seasonal ecology of the semi-desert lands of the Horn of Africa. Thus it was not implied that Britain or anyone else might be empowered to alienate any part of that territory - quite the reverse - or to restrict the vital patterns of transhumance. But this they did, without the consent or even the knowledge of the Somali inhabitants.[3]

European imperialism in Africa rested on agreements between involved powers - sometimes before actual penetration, sometimes in the course of it. Treaties were drawn up dividing territory and delineating boundaries. As often as not these disregarded existing African political units altogether. At other times such polities were divided up with little regard to the political allegiances of the population. In other words, the scramble marked off territory solely in terms of rights claimed under international law as agreed between involved powers. Although the Somalis and others were locally slow to comprehend this, one of the greatest achievements of the Ethiopian Emperor Menelik II and his advisers was his success in having Ethiopia recognised as one of the powers whose 'rights' - resting, of course, on often bloody imperialist expansion - were taken into account in the wider world. He also played on Abyssinia's ancient form of Christianity to acquire superior fire-power, with which to subjugate his African neighbours, including the Oromo and Somalis, and in the event, to defend himself against Egyptian and Italian expansionism.[4]

Legal questions concerning the effective control of acquired territory and the continuation of resistance are important. This is particularly so since one of the territories Menelik sought to acquire - the Ogaden - bordered on areas also inhabited by Somalis but already under the flags of other powers: Britain, Italy and France. 'Effective control' was prized by them because it was one of the conditions laid down by the 1885 Berlin Act to support a claim to territory; for reasons of economy; and because of the ideological imperatives of the 'imperial mission' - peace, prosperity and, perhaps, improvement. Arbitrary frontiers were imposed. Supposed rights under international law always discourage intervention but, more important, they spread a cloud of mystification over the actual allegiances of the people themselves. Meantime, in international law, although new states are held to inherit frontier agreements, there has been growing emphasis on the primacy of the right to self-determination. Herein is the nub of the contradiction posed by the Ogaden or Western Somalia.

In 1887 Menelik occupied Harar and in 1891 announced an ambitious programme of Abyssinian expansion and colonisation to the European powers. Further Abyssinian moves included somewhat tentative, but nevertheless bloody and brutal, expansion into the Ogaden and elsewhere, including lands where, it should be noted, the Somalis had already signed or were in the process of signing protectorate treaties with one or other European power.

Britain considered that her main interests lay on the Somali coast and in the Sudan. Her representatives visiting Addis Ababa were thus willing in 1897 to divide with Menelik the lands of Somali groups in the interior, even those with which Britain had pre-existing treaties, a division conditional only on Menelik's agreement that those Somalis would be properly governed and afforded their traditional grazing rights. Italy was at the time similarly insensitive over the Ogaden. (She later revised her attitude, perhaps not only, but at least partly, because of her expansionist plans under Benito Mussolini.) After her southward expansion from northern Eritrea had been halted by defeat at the hands of the Ethiopians at Adowa, Menelik was invited to draw a line on a map marking a boundary between Italian Somaliland and Ethiopia. This agreement was later 'lost' although it is sketchily referred to in a 1908 treaty between Ethiopia and Italy. Thus that frontier too, known as 'the provisional administrative line', has never been formally defined, let alone demarcated.[5]

The Somalis, it should be emphasised, quite apart from not being consulted over these or any subsequent agreements between European powers and Ethiopia, resisted all parties, including (even especially) the Amhara. Ever since the 1890s all Somalis have considered themselves victims of a great injustice - even conspiracy is not too strong a word. Ethiopian administration of the Ogaden was sketchy in the extreme in the period up to the outbreak of war with Italy in 1935; sporadic tax 'raids' were sent out often without success but resident Ethiopian administrators and military personnel resided only in the major northern townships of Harar and Jigjiga. Indeed, the 1934 flashpoint of the conflict with Italy - the celebrated Wal-Wal incident -was indicative of the sparseness of the Ethiopian presence. By chance an Italian garrison was found by a boundary commission to have been established well inside Ethiopian territory - its commanding officer claimed that it had been there several years - and the Ethio - Italian war, which preceded World War II, ensued.

After Italy had defeated the Emperor Haile Sellassie's armies in 1936, she administered the Ogaden as an integral part of Italian Somali and. During World War II, Italy also occupied the British Somaliland Protectorate and even after victory in the Horn of Africa in 1941-2, British Commonwealth forces retained the administration of the main Somali-populated areas within Ethiopia, in several areas right up until 1954. Not surprisingly pan-Somali feeling flourished. In particular, political and cultural organisations, notably the Somali Youth League, blossomed in a benevolent atmosphere and even colonial military or para-military forces, such as the Somalia gendarmerie became renowned for their nationalist consciousness. Somali nationalism was rife not only in the 'British' and 'Italian' Somalilands but also in Western Somalia and north-eastern Kenya. The restoration of 'legality', i.e. the reinstatement of locally contested but internationally recognised Ethiopian sovereignty, was challenged by the concept of 'Greater' or 'United' Somalia. This is very apparent from reports, petitions, and a number of incidents in the late 1940s, including serious disturbances in Harar. It was in any case the era of decolonisation throughout Asia and Africa.[6]

The arrival in the Ogaden in 1947 of a prospecting team of an American oil company, Sinclair Petroleum, with a 50-year concession throughout the Ethiopian empire granted by Haile Sellassie, fanned Somali opposition to the return of Ethiopian 'administration'. The prospectors were stoned and forced to withdraw temporarily in January 1948. At the same time this forced the British military administration to concede that the strength of Somali nationalist feeling among its only available armed forces was such that any attempt to give protection to the oilmen might result in armed risings throughout all the Somali territories under British administration.[7]

An overview of the situation by the Vice-Chief of the Imperial General Staff in the British War Office was also a sound prediction of future events. He reported in January 1948 - and his second paragraph is particularly noteworthy - as follows:

'The one thing that the Somalis will not tolerate at any price is that the Ogaden should revert to Ethiopia. It appears that they would be quite content if the Ogaden together with Italian Somaliland were placed under British trusteeship. They might tolerate, but with considerable reluctance and probably a display of some violence, trusteeship going to Italy; but there will undoubtedly by very great disturbances if the Ogaden is awarded to Ethiopia.

'The Somalis do not object to the Sinclair Oil Company as such, although I believe its employees do not always conduct themselves with great tact. It is a fact that their concession has been granted by the Emperor of Ethiopia and that their authority to prospect comes from him - this is the cause of the trouble.'[8]

No oil find was announced, but paradoxically some Somalis benefited from water boreholes drilled by the prospectors. Administration of most of the Ogaden reverted to Ethiopia in September 1948. Later, Italy was granted a ten year United Nations trusteeship over her former Somali territories, to expire in 1960. Meantime the Somali Youth League continued to expand its activities throughout the Somali lands and called for cultural and political freedom. In 1954-5, when the Haud and other areas still reserved to the British were being taken over by Ethiopia, violent demonstrations again occurred. The Somali Youth League was proscribed by the Ethiopians and an attempt was made to ban all political activity. Tens of thousands of refugees fled from the Ethiopian military and a long refugee saga was initiated which was to reach crescendo in 1979-81, with more than two million refugees and displaced persons in the wider region. It was still a problem at the end of the decade.

In 1978 the then leader of the resistance movement that inevitably had grown up in the Ogaden, commented:

'The liberation struggle of the Somali people in Western Somalia is the same historical struggle for independence as that fought by Ahmad Gurey in the past; as that of Sayyid Muhammad Abdille Hassan and as that of the Somali Youth League (SYL). Its translation into the present movement - the Western Somali Liberation Front (WSLF) - is the most recent phase. The Liberation Front developed in 1963 from the Nasar Allah movement in that part of the Somali country where Ethiopian colonialism, and consequently the armed struggle, still continues. It is only the level of intensity of the People's struggle that has increased since 1963.'[9]

A provisional administrative line, running along the border between the Ogaden and former Italian Somaliland was established by Britain, Ethiopia and Italy early in 1950 after considerable negotiation which, nevertheless, ignored local Somali opinion.[10] Repeated United Nations efforts to secure the demarcation of a boundary between Ethiopia and Somalia from 1950 to 1960, as well as the language of the Trusteeship Agreement itself, make it clear that the UN did not believe that the provisional administrative line of 1950 was a legal or *de jure* border.[11] The Italian Government also made every effort to solve the problem by negotiation. It is a matter of record at the UN that the Ethiopian Government did not co-operate, possibly in the hope that she might annex Somalia as she was to annex Eritrea. Instead, Somalia became independent in 1960 and at once united with the former British Protectorate which had achieved independence a few days earlier. For the next 25 years, disputes between the Somali Republic and Ethiopia were repeatedly tabled before the OAU Council of Ministers and Heads of State and Government meetings. A pattern of friction and confrontation also typified UN meetings in New York and Geneva.

When, due to negligence, incompetence and corruption in Ethiopia - which also triggered the 1974 'revolution' in that country - adequate measures were not taken to deal with famines which struck parts of north-eastern Africa and the Sahel, and attempts were even made to cover up the starvation and suffering of the people, Western Somali resistance escalated. The Somali Government responded with the provision of food and supplies. Refugees and resettlement camps were established within Somalia. Even so, early in 1977 the people of Western Somalia rose in rebellion.

The Government of the Somali Democratic Republic had long restrained militants in the Somali Armed Forces and elsewhere - particularly in 1974, when Major-General Mohamed Siad Barre was Chairman of the OAU - but pressure from citizens in Somalia, especially those who had themselves been born in Ethiopian administered areas, increased.[12]

Encouraged by disarray within Ethiopia, it reached the point where the Somali Government could restrain it no further. Advice counselling restraint was rejected and Somali Government forces overran the Ogaden, halting only at the outskirts of Harar and Dira Dawa. It was at this point that the Soviet Union and Cuba intervened decisively. More than 250 heavy military transport aircraft, mainly Antonov 22s but including a fleet of Tupolev 76s, and some civil aircraft took part in airlifts of men and material on a hitherto unprecedented scale.[13] The Ogaden was recaptured by largely Ethio-Cuban forces directed by senior Russian officers, but an avenue was left for the remnants of the Somali army to withdraw - probably by arrangement between the superpowers.

As Ethiopian military occupation was restored and massive refugee flows again ensued, [14] there were frequent incidents between 1978-82, involving the land and air forces of Ethiopia and the Somali Democratic Republic. Slowly, the Somalis managed to infiltrate their armed forces back into the Ogaden, but they were later obliged to withdraw them again, following American pressure.

Overnight on 30 June 1982 Socialist Ethiopia's forces crossed the provisional administrative line - which, although a *de facto* border had for many years marked the limit of the south-western expansion of Haile Sellassie's empire - and invaded the Somali Democratic Republic.[15]

The Present Situation

The public attitude of contemporary Ethiopia towards the dispute with the Somali Democratic Republic is legalistic. While she admits that the provisional administrative line is not an agreed international frontier she maintains that any dispute is over its exact position, i.e. there is a boundary dispute. She bases all her arguments on international laws of succession and seeks merely to establish where exactly the line agreed between Menelik and Italy lies. On this she would be prepared to negotiate. Ethiopia actively and to date successfully campaigns for OAU support, arguing that to adjust any African boundaries would be to invite continent-wide chaos. Privately, however, there are still influential Amhara who would like to annexe Djibouti and the Somali Democratic Republic.

The position of the Somali Democratic Republic on the other hand is based on the overriding principle of self-determination for non-self-governing peoples, amongst whom she would include the population of Western Somalia or the Ogaden - and others, including the Eritreans. The Somali Government and the Western Somali Liberation Front (WSLF) regarded the expansion of Abyssinia and the creation of the modern Ethiopian empire during the scramble for Africa and since as 'black colonialism'. The Somali view is that the populations there, too, have as much right to choose their allegiance and system of government as had the citizens of former British and Italian Somalilands (now the Somali Democratic Republic) and French Somaliland (now the Republic of Djibouti)[16] who were in fact colonised somewhat earlier, but who are now independent. The Somali Government thus recognise a territorial rather than a boundary dispute.

Clearly the Somali Government, which after independence had openly proclaimed its ambition to unite all territories inhabited by Somalis, hope that given the right of self-determination, the population of Western Somalia would opt to unite with the Republic. This is by no means certain however, since the views of the peoples of Western Somalia have not been ascertained even to the extent that they were in the case of the Somalia in what was formerly the Northern Frontier District or Province of Kenya.[17] There are other subject peoples within Ethiopia who could conceivably one day settle for the decentralisation of government from Addis Ababa.

The location of the OAU headquarters to Addis Ababa and the early predominance of Ethiopians on its staff have greatly assisted the projection of 'Ethiopian' interests in that body. Thus, although the Charter of the OAU makes no mention of international boundaries, referring merely to 'territorial integrity', the Ethiopians have managed to secure the proposal and acceptance of a ruling at the Heads of State Conference in Cairo, 1964, safeguarding the permanence of boundaries inherited on the achievement of independence. In point of fact this decision specifically excluded the Ogaden issue but in 1980 the Ethiopians supported by the Nigerians and others managed to have this ruling applied to the Ogaden.[18] The Somalis, as usual, reserved their position but it constituted a diplomatic defeat within the context of the OAU.

The Government of Somalia recognised the independence of Djibouti. She has also drawn a fine distinction between the Somali-inhabited areas of Kenya and those within Ethiopia on the grounds that the Kenyans themselves never actually colonised Somali regions as the Amhara did. The OAU ruling on the inviolability of frontiers inherited from the colonial period, therefore, would, according to Somalia, only appertain in the case of the Ogaden subsequent to its decolonisation.

The United Nations has not taken a clear position but definitions of aggression specifically exclude assistance to colonised peoples. The predominant Ethiopian view at the United Nations, however, as at the OAU, is that colonisation is a phenomenon involving Europeans and not inter-African relationships. The Somalis have no 'recognised' liberation movements. Moreover, the United Nations for years failed to support self-determination for Eritrea despite having established that country as a self-governing entity by a 1950 decision of the General Assembly.[19] (Ethiopia subsequently annexed what should have been a self-governing part of a federation between the two nations.)

Today the Ethiopian Government denies having any territorial ambition in Somalia, conveniently ignoring claims which have been made on several occasions over the years:[20] the Somalis likewise with regard to the Ogaden. Each, however, sought to enlist the assistance and support of one or other super power - Ethiopia arguably achieving greater success first with the United States and then with the Soviet Union. In 1990, the United States appeared once more to incline towards Ethiopia - but real issues are not yet being addressed at grass-roots level, however. For lasting peace the people must needs be consulted - when that happens there could well be many surprises. But, in this context, a caution: the outcome of tactical moves either by outside powers or by local dictators should never be confused with the resolution of deep seated conflicts of interest. The Mengistu regime in Ethiopia sought to use conflicts within Somalia - as it did conflicts (the use of the word 'contradictions' is doubtless now passé) within the Sudan. Somalia likewise: with measurably less expertise, Somalia exploited the resentments of the suppressed nationalities and the injustices visited on the Eritreans. Her efforts were mainly frustrated or rendered incoherent by differences of opinion between the President and his half-brother, for a long period Minister of Foreign Affairs, and the external operations departments of the Intelligence (the NSS) on the one hand, and most western educated ministers, diplomats and advisers on the other. That the latter were heard at all is probably only because they had the sympathetic ear of one of the President's sons in law, who was a long time intelligence chief.

Even so, uprisings in the Sudan, in Eritrea, Ethiopia and Somalia all have their own dynamic. Only a leader schooled narrowly in intrigue and Machievellian strictures on divide and rule, would fail to appreciate the very real grass roots support for these movements. Sudan cannot order the Eritrean 'resistance' to desist; nor can Ethiopia (or Israel) do anything more than hinder the pattern of change in the Sudanese provinces. Ethiopia has sought to take advantage of clan rivalries in Somalia, for they have undoubtedly been significant in liberation struggles. Whilst Siad Barre's police threw the office furniture of the WSLF into the road, the SNM surprised their 'keepers' by taking the civil war across the border into Northern Somalia in May 1989, without Ethiopia's prior approval.

Just as Ethiopia could encourage but not control the Somali demand for an end to dictatorship and repression - not just on the part of the largely but not entirely Isak SNM, but also the largely Hawiya USC and the SPM, in the main drawn from Ogadeen clansmen within the Somali Democratic Republic - so Siad Barre could not create permanent enmity between clans which he felt no longer supported his junta. He encouraged the clans of the north to fight each other, with promises of bribes, investment and arms. He encouraged the deprived refugees from Western Somalia - both Somali and Oromo - to seize the property of the rebellions Isak in and around Hargeisa and elsewhere. But such tactics, although they made for temporary enmity, only obscured the real problems for a short period. The old truism about the possibility of fooling all of the people all of the time is most relevant here. Somali culture is quite homogeneous and can prove strong enough to heal these wounds naturally, but it will take time.

Alternatively - and dangerously - if a new national leader has to stress the unity of the nation, recent history suggests, as in Ethiopia in 1977, it could be done at the expense of traditional enemies or, as in Iran, by harnessing religious extremism. It is vital, therefore, to heed the grass roots voices rather than the old dictators. In Kenya the Commander of the Army, the Minister in charge of Intelligence, the Provisional Commissioner of the important Rift Valley Province are all Kenyan Somalis. There are by contrast no Ogaden Somali voices in Ethiopia's corridors of power, and, moreover, there is no development. As one Ogaden voice charitably put it - 'at least we owe the IMF and the World Bank nothing!' Ethiopian Somalis are second or third class citizens - except of course in pre-civil war Somalia - and the détente of 1986-90 between Mengistu and Siad Barre is irrelevant to them. Yet again, they are neither consulted nor understood, but their aspirations are a reality which will not go away.

Meantime, it is not only the African neighbours of the ailing states of the Horn of Africa who have to share the disruption and the immense fiscal and human costs of military confrontations and resultant refugee flows. Is it perhaps time for a new initiative involving all the populations of the Horn of Africa? A time to co-operate and encourage an agreed solution which takes into account views and aspirations of all the population of all the affected areas? It worked eventually in Zimbabwe (which was 'colonised' before the Ogaden). The fighting stopped. And the refugees went home. And environmental and development problems could at last begin to be addressed.

---

1   Cerulli is sometimes misquoted, 'a museum of peoples'.

2   For a useful recent discussion of the history of the Horn of Africa in 'medieval' times see Taddesse Tamrat, 'Ethiopia, the Red Sea and the Horn' in Roland Oliver (ed.) *The Cambridge History of Africa* 3, (Cambridge, 1977), pp 98-182.

3   For typical British treaties with Somali clans see, for example, Public Record Office, London (PRO) FO 844/1. French and Italian treaties of a similar type are reproduced, for example, by Information Services of the Somali Government, *The Somali Peninsula. A New Light on Imperial Motives* (Mogadishu, 1962), Appendices I(b)); VI(d), VI(e).

4   Recent scholarship increasingly stresses Menelik's 'imperialism' rather than his 'defensive expansionism'. See, for example, Harold G Marcus, 'Imperialism and Expansionism in Ethiopia from 1865 to 1900' in Lewis Gann and Peter Duigan (eds) *Colonialism in Africa.* 1, (Cambridge, 1969), pp 420-61 and Bonnie Holcomb and Sisai Ibssa, *The Invention of Ethiopia.* (Trenton, NJ 1990), pp 88 157 and passim.

5   Ibid Leo Silberman, 'Why the Haud was Ceded' *Cahiers D'Etudes Africaines* 2, No. 1 (1961), pp 37-81 is also 'crucial. For the Italio-Ethiopian agreements see, for example, A Gingold Duprey, *De L'Invasion a la Liberation de L'Ethiopie.* 1, (Paris, 1955) p. 49, 98-9, and Annexe T.30 (p. 430). For the 'provisional administrative line' see note 10 and 11 below, and p.7 of the text.

6   Pan-Somali nationalism and its recognition in British plans for a 'Greater Somalia' in the 1940s are well-documented in British Colonial Office, Foreign Office and War Office files in the Public Record Office. Lack of space precludes full citation here.

7   On the Somali reaction to Sinclair Petroleum operations in the Ogaden see, for example, PRO FO 1015/83; FO 371/69295,69296, 69297.

8   Minute by VCIGS, 23 January 1948, PRO FO 1015/83.

9   Quoted in Ministry of Foreign Affairs, Somali Democratic Republic, *Go From My Country: Western Somalia and Abyssinian Colonialism* (Mogadishu, 1978), p.2. See also, *West Africa.* No. 3160, 6 February 1978.

10   For the negotiations leading to the establishment of the 'provisional administrative line' see, for example, PRO FO 1015/548, 549; and WO 230/296, which contains Somali petitions protesting at the position of the line.

11   For a summary of UN efforts to secure the demarcation of the Ethiopia-Somalia border between 1950 and 1960 see *Yearbook of the United, Nations*. 1950, p.372, 1951, pp.692-3; 1952, pp. 629-30; 1953, p. 604; 1954, pp.393-8; 1955, pp 324-5; 1956, pp 344-5; 1957, pp.333-5; 1958, pp. 344-6; 1959, pp.358-9.

12   Ogaden-born Somalis are to be found in significant numbers in most government ministries in Mogadishu and are also influential in the armed forces and the ruling party - the SRSP. The term Ogaden derives from the Ogadeen, a Somali clan who are not the sole inhabitants of the area - indeed, in former times, the British War Office referred to the area as 'Abyssinian Somaliland'. The Ethiopian authorities in the early 1980s changed certain boundaries to restrict the use of the term Ogaden, very possibly as a safeguard in case they one day had to surrender it or recognise the wishes of its population.

13   Special satellites were launched to guide the airlift and gather intelligence. The materials supplied included ground-to-ground missiles, howitzer batteries, Stalin-organs (40 122 BM-21 rocket launchers mounted on Ural 375 trucks) and other artillery, T55 and T62 tanks, radar towers and mobile radar equipment, airfield construction equipment and electric fencing, Sukhoi fighter bombers, MiG 21s and 23s, helicopter gunships and massive quantities of fuel, rockets and ammunition.

14   Richard Greenfield, 'The Current Refugee Situation in North East Africa - a Problem in Afro-Arab Relations?' in *Symposium on Afro-Arab Relations in the Eighties. Cairo. 21-24 January 1980*, (Arab League Secretariat Cairo, 1980) and 'An Historial Introduction to Refugee Problems in the Horn', Horn of Africa, 2, No 4 (1979), pp.14-26.

15   The Ogaden conflict of 1977-78, and earlier clashes have been described in much available literature. That is not the case in this instance, but see Richard Greenfield, 'Africa's New Flash-points' *New African* No 180, September 1982; and 'The Spreading War for a Wasteland' *Newsweek*. 30 August 1982, p.47. There follows an outline of what took place, which was to prove an important bargaining counter in 1986-90 when both the Ethiopian and the Somali dictators found themselves in desparate need of their respective troops in other theatres:
Incursions took place at several points. The first was launched from Ferfer, an 'Ethiopian' border settlement of strategic importance - sometimes known as the 'gateway to the Ogaden'. An obvious first intention of the Ethiopian forces was to capture high land near the Ferfer township. Heavy ground and air attacks were made but the Ethiopians were repulsed with quite heavy losses in men and material, by the Somali garrison at Belet Uen. A stalemate ensued. Had this high land been occupied, however, it would have afforded Ethiopian artillery and mortars a 'beaten zone' covering both the only arterial road to the north and the road link east to the capital, Mogadishu. Effectively Somalia would have been cut in half.
Further north another Ethiopian armoured column overran the Somali settlement of Balambale on 10 July 1982 and then advanced a further 11 km. A counter-attack was soon organised by the Somali Divisional Operations Commander based at El dere and the Ethiopians were contained 3 km from Balambale, which settlement they held and fortified.
The forces involved were the Ethiopian 8th Mechanised Infantry Division consisting of three mechanised brigades, some 30 to 45 T55 tanks; two artillery battalions armed with D-30 122 mm high velocity heavy howitzers; two mortar batteries, each with eight pieces; a reconnaissance group and other support units - in all some 8,000 to 10,000 men. Some 29 Ethiopian prisoners, including two officers, one of whom was wounded, were captured by the Somalis in 1982.
Still further north, the airstrip and other parts of the provincial capital of Galcaio were strafed by Ethiopian planes - several flights of MiG 21s and one Ilyushin fighter bomber. The bombs used created deep craters on impact but they missed the airport runway. Not all exploded. Rockets were also employed but they too missed their targets - the air defence emplacements. Unexploded bombs and rocket casings bore Russian markings. The runway at Galcaio, which was in the process of being extended, was undamaged.

112

Ethiopian armoured columns also crossed the *'de facto'* border to the north and west of Galcaio. They overran the small Somali settlement of Guldogob. The original intention appears to have been to breach the north-south arterial road and thus also to divide the country, but this advance was held and the Ethiopian forces, although reinforced from Warder, pulled back and dug in as they did at Balambale. The Ethiopian 11th Division remained poised north of Galcaio, with three mechanised brigades and between 45 and 60 T54 and perhaps T55 tanks, two artillery battalions with D30s, one artillery battalion with D17 130 mm guns, two mortar batteries with eight pieces each and reconnaissance and support teams.

There were limited confrontations at several other points further north but at no time were foreign troops - or even the few hundred Somali dissidents known to be present - engaged in actual fighting in 1982. Even so, there is little doubt of Soviet, Cuban, South Yemeni and Libyan involvement, apparently confined to divisional level.

Phials of Russian-made poison-gas-testing chemicals with instructions in Russian were also found in the possession of captured Ethiopians. Somali army officers claimed to have intercepted radio traffic involving air support in Russian (ground-to-air) and Spanish (air-to-air) - the latter implying Cuban participation. There was also some indirect evidence of Soviet tactical control since, untypically, Ethiopian troop movements were followed by helicopters.

Initially the Somalis had only 1,800 men in the region where hostilities broke out but these were soon reinforced. In the last month of 1982, consignments of light arms including anti-tank and anti-aircraft weapons were also received. These were mainly from the United States. US tanks were also shipped, but from Italy. Towards the end of 1982 a consignment of MiGs arrived from China to reinforce the Somali airforce decimated in the 1978 conflict, but Somali troops enjoyed next to no air support.

16 At the suggestion of the late Emperor Haile Sellassie, President Charles de Gaulle agreed to change the name of present-day Djibouti from 'French Somaliland' to 'The Territory of the Afars and Issas'.

17 For consultations in the Northern Frontier District in 1962 see *Kenya: Report of the Northern Frontier District Commission*, Cmd. 1900 (1962); and for background and interpretation of it, A A Castagno, 'The Somali-Kenyan Controversy: Implications for the Future', *Journal of Modern African Studies*, 2, No. 2 (1964), pp. 165-88.

18 See the official record of the 1964 Cairo OAU Summit which clearly shows that this resolution was intended to apply only to new disputes *vide* Chairman Sekou Toure's summary: 'What is required is that this Conference re-affirm the principles contained in the Charter and these discussions do not concern disputes which exist now...', and the comments of the Ethiopian Prime Minister '... in my humble opinion, there is no connection between this resolution and the dispute obtaining between Somalia and Ethiopia...' The Ogaden issue was already before the OAU in 1964. The OAU Good Offices Committee meeting in Lagos in 1981, took a different view, see Doc. AHG/105 (xviii) Annes 11, and its acceptance, with certain reservations by Somalia and Djibouti, at the 1981 Nairobi Summit.

19 For the UN's own celebration of its creation of Eritrea see *shaping a People's Destiny - the Story of Eritrea and the United Nations* (New York: UN Dept of Public Information, 1951).

20 For Ethiopian claims to the former Italian Somaliland after World War II i.e. territory *beyond* the Ogaden - see, for example, 'Memorandum' dd. 8 September 1945, enclosure in Aklilou (Ethiopian Vice-Minister of Foreign Affairs) to RFG Sarell, British Charge d'Affaires, Addis Ababa, 8 September 1945; 'Memorandum No I from the Imperial Ethiopian Government' (to the Conference of Foreign Ministers - the 'Big Four') dd. 28 September 1945, J3481 in FO 371 /46114. Bitwoded Makonnen Makonnen Endalkatchew (Prime Minister of Ethiopia) to H McNeil, MP (other copies were sent, *inter alia* to the British Prime Minister, Clement Attlee; *The Times*; and *The Guardian*), 12 February 1946, J1083 in 371/53465. See also the response of Margery Perham in a letter to *The Times* 12 March 1946. Cf. 'Ethiopian Development', *The Economist*, 7 December 1946.

10 Somalia: Federalism and Self-Determination

HUSSEIN M ADAM

Issues such as confederation, federation, autonomy and decentralisation have become important to contemporary Somali politics. All this is partly a reaction to the Siad Barre dictatorship which was militarist, centralist and brutal. At least the two opposition groups that are currently holding power in the north (the Somali National Movement - SNM) and the south (United Somali Congress - USC) of Somalia have advocated for federalism and decentralisation in their relatively recent constitutions and official documents. Few scholars recall that the case for a federal system for Somalia was first raised in 1947.

Federalism and Somali Nationalism

Somalis are reputed to share the same language, religion, physical features and culture as the most homogeneous people in Africa. Stereotypical images about the Somalis have led scholars to ignore key differences among them. In spite of homogeneity and the pain of the multiple partitions, the Somali nationalist movement was always divided, manifesting itself in multiple parties. Unlike TANU which dominated the scene in British Tanganyika between 1954-1961, for British Somaliland there were four, and for Italian Somaliland there were at least ten political parties.[1] One reason for this is due to the fluid nature of clanism and the ability of the elites to politicise its various segments; the other is the pastoral and agro-pastoral tradition of independence that resents uniformity.

114

Following the Italian defeat during World War II, most of the Horn of Africa (Eritrea, Ethiopia, Somalia), came under the British Military Administration (BMA). The main nationalist party in ex-Italian Somaliland then was the Somali Youth League (SYL).

Between 1946 and 1948, the BMA in Somalia (1941-1950) supported the SYL and gave it valuable assistance. One of the ways it did this was by providing SYL members with jobs and administrative experience. The majority of the Somalis who were employed in the BMA administration, whether in military service or civilian administration, came from the SYL.[2]

Though nationalist, the SYL at that point in time was dominated mostly by Hawiye (Somali clan-family), and Darod (another clan-family) elites.

The elites of the clan-family inhabiting the area between the two rivers, the Shabelle and Juba Rivers, saw the British giving unfair advantages to others. Thus they formed their own party in order to redress the process of class formation to make it at least less skewed against their own group. They formed the Hizbia Dighil Mirifle (HDM), the part of their clan-family, the Dighil Mirifle. Later on they realised that the issue of decentralisation they raised applied to others in Somalia as well, and they renamed their party the Hizb al-Dastuur Mustaqil al-Somal (HDMS), Somali Independent Constitutional Party.

This discussion pertains to ex-Italian Somaliland and the north-south differences mentioned below should be taken in that context:

To 'Hizbia' the country of (Italian) Somaliland was divided into two major regions: north of the Shabelle River and south of it, speaking two noticeably different dialects, 'maai' in the south, 'mahaatiri' in the north. The 'Hizbia' people practice mixed farming and pastoralism in the prosperous region of Somalia. Thus, there are important economic, cultural and linguistic differences between the southern population and the predominantly nomadic people of the north.[3]

Since there is a dialectical relationship between clan (ethnicity) and class formation issues, it is not surprising to find an outwardly clan-family party, the HDMS, fighting against alleged discrimination of Dighil-Mirifle citizens in the process of Somalization of the civil service and armed forces and in the allocation of educational scholarships for study abroad. They also struggled against government attempts to impose heavy taxes on their farms. Mukhtar concludes his analysis of HDMS politics thus:

'While there is a common and deeply-rooted belief in Somali society that all Somalis are descended from a single ancestor, there is little doubt that geography and history have created several distinct sub-cultures within Somalia...The HDMS was accused of being a tribal party, though they, in fact, represented for more than 20 years (1947-1969) the sole opposition party, especially in the period preceding independence. They raised important issues in Somali political development, such as: the necessity of undertaking a consensus of the Somali population as a basic step of development, the vitality of 'al-Dastuur' (the constitution) as a sole way to a democratic political entity and the adoption of a federal system of government as the only way that Somaliland could be developed economically and socially.'[4]

This is but one example of how a clan-family that fears actual and/or potential domination project themselves into a party and thus seek through it to control their own lives and advance their condition. Clanism is obviously generated as a compensatory reaction. Years ago Frantz Fanon noticed a similar phenomenon when he observed, 'we find in underdeveloped countries fierce demands for social justice which paradoxically are allied with often primitive tribalism.'[5]

Opposition Movements and Federalism

In the area of the former HDMS, an anti-Siad opposition movement has grown up, the Somali Democratic Movement (SDM). Unlike the HDMS, the SDM does not have to apologise for its clan-family basis - today all the Somali opposition parties share the same characteristic. The SDM began as a political movement, but it has had to fight remnants of the Siad forces and it has, therefore, been forced to create armed wings. The SDM is somewhat divided between old guard leaders of the HDMS and an energetic group of 'young Turks.' Its representatives at the recent Djibouti conferences on Somalia and at other meetings emphasised the issue of federalism as the best way to avoid conflicts among Somalis.

The first armed opposition group to rise against the Siad military dictatorship followed the failure of the April 1978 military coup d'état. The officers who fled Somalia after the coup to seek political asylum in Ethiopia later formed the Somali Salvation Democratic Front (SSDF). A sub-branch of the Mijertain clan (Darod clan-family) was involved. Siad moved to co-opt the rest of the clan and the SSDF was never able to expand its base. By the mid-eighties he was able to divide and entice the bulk of the SSDF fighters to return and fight in the north and in Mogadishu under Siad's Darod hegemony (clan family involving Siad's Marehan, Mijertain, Dulbahante, Ogaden, Warsangeli clans). SSDF documents talked about the old parliamentary democracy (1960-69), as the ideal political system in the future. It is vague on the issue of securing political participation as well as on federalism and decentralisation.

In a London meeting in April 1981, the Somali National Movement (SNM) was born. It drew its support mainly from the Isaaq clan-family of ex-British Somaliland. However, for a time the vice-chairman of the SNM was Ali Mohamed 'Wardigley', a Hawiye, who later moved on to found the United Somali Congress (USC) based on the Hawiye clan-family of north-central and central Somalia including the capital city, Mogadishu. Siad moved at full speed to persecute the Isaaq while the SNM developed in a short time into an efficient and strong military movement. In 1988 Siad Signed a peace treaty with Ethiopia's Mengistu hoping that it would lead to a disarming of the SNM. The SNM decided to launch a full-scale war against Siad's forces in the north. The Siad army launched indiscriminate air and ground attacks. The violence and brutality pushed most people to embrace the SNM.

'The outbreak of the civil war in the North signalled the beginning of a collapse of the Mogadishu Government. Although the Government succeeded in gaining the support of several minor clans and/or movements in the North, the persistence of the SNM units hindered the Government attempts to regain full control over the North. During 1989 and 1990 only the main cities, such as Hargeisa, Burao and Berbera remained under the Government control.'6

As of mid-1988, the SNM possessed liberated zones analysed by Basil Davidson as 'a proof of a nationalist fighting movement's efficacy, a demonstration of what is to come after victory, but also a vital means of achieving that victory'.7

In a series of documents published before the SNM declaration of independence in May 1991, the movement proposed that Somalia be divided into regions with elected governors and regional assemblies. Each region would have its own development plan, administrative system, and judicial apparatus (in uniformity with the other regions). Regional governments would take charge of key social services such as health, education up to the university level, electricity, roads and public transport. The SNM proposes a policy of local staff recruitment and autonomy partially as an antidote to corruption. The sense of living in and belonging to a particular community can enhance public service accountability. Also, this trenchant regional/local approach reflects deeply felt Somali political values such as fairness, equality, proportionality especially with regards to clan development and class formation as shown in the case of the HDMS of 40 years ago. Partly to offset the tendency for the central state to control all external and internal resources, the SNM programme during the years of struggle states: 'The finances of the central government will come from tax levies on the region's resources of revenues, and will be a fraction of the revenues of the regions to be stipulated in the future.'8

The financial stipulations are not only substantive in establishing viable federal systems, they also can play indirect roles in reducing the stakes in national election outcomes. Federal pluralist democracy might enhance moderation and restraint thereby promoting democratic stability. The United Somali Congress (USC) was launched in early 1989 and has held three party Congresses so far. It is a young movement that is still growing politically. Militarily, it was successful in getting the Siad regime to collapse in Mogadishu by January 1991. Like the SNM and the other opposition movements, it advocates 'a multi-party democracy based on true representation and full participation of the people of Somalia.'9 With regards to federalism, the USC echoes points elaborated by the SNM above:

The USC shall formulate national policies, strategies and plan of action to effectively establish and consolidate a Federal Central Government and democratically elected parliament that truly represents all the Somali citizens; as well as establish the principle of Regional self-government. This will help create a systematic decentralisation of governmental institutions and support local planning and decision-making, community initiative and participation which will eventually lead to the people's self-reliance in all aspects of their political, social and economic lives.10

The Most Violent of Transitions

Recent African transitions from military dictatorships or authoritarian civilian one-party regime towards relatively democratic trends have taken various forms. In Benin, Togo and other countries, a National Conference served as the catalyst for the transition. Riots, strikes and other forms of mass disturbance obliged the regimes in power to accept the National Conference and its outcomes. In other countries, Zambia for example, regime change came about as a result of free and fair democratic elections. In several African countries, the ruling elites continue to guide the democratisation process by co-opting or hijacking the transition process through false promises and piecemeal reforms. In Uganda, Liberia and Somalia, the transition has come about through armed insurrections culminating in violent civil wars.

From 1960-69, Somalia operated a multi-party parliamentary system. The constitution and electoral law, drafted by foreign experts, did not take into account the pastoral democratic traditions based on power sharing concepts. These top-down imposed 'democratic' mechanisms pushed competition to the point of conflicts, inflamed clan and sub-clan rivalries resulting in periods of anarchy followed by government paralysis. Soon after the chaotic 1969 elections, the Somali National Army staged a coup and General Mohamed Siad Barre installed himself as the new ruler. As a consequence of conflicts with the U.S.-armed Ethiopian army, the Somali military sought and obtained USSR military assistance from 1964. In time, it grew into a formidable fighting machine, one of the very best in sub-Saharan Africa.

During his early years in power, Siad proclaimed 'scientific socialism' and carried out self-help schemes including, a major rural development campaign, an expansion of schooling, and a campaign to combat moving sand dunes. In 1972, the Somali language was reduced to a written form utilising an adapted Latin script. This was followed by an urban and rural mass literacy campaign - the latter constituting the major aspect of the rural development campaign. In 1977, Siad unleashed the Somali army to back guerrillas of the Western Somali Liberation Front in a major war with Mengistu's revolutionary Ethiopia. The USSR backed Ethiopia as Siad broke the treaty of friendship with the USSR and allied himself with the U.S. under President Carter. The USSR gave Ethiopia huge amounts of arms and logistical support and thousands of Cuban troops were airlifted to defeat the Somali army in the Ogaden. Divisions within Somali society led to an attempted coup and the birth of the first armed opposition group based in Ethiopia as mentioned above.

The Siad regime began to manifest a neofascist face. For a considerable period it unleashed its brutality on the Isaaq clan family in the former British Somaliland. By the time the regime fell in 1991, it had managed to destroy most of the northern cities (Hargeisa, Burao), towns (Gebile) and major villages. The Siad military dictatorship intensified the politicisation of clan-family and clan identities. He struggled to impose a Darod hegemony in the hope of prolonging his regime's hold on power. I. M. Lewis has this to say:

...male Ogadeni refugees in Northern Somalia, who have long been subject to illegal recruitment into Somalia's armed forces have been conscripted as a paramilitary militia to fight the SNM and man checkpoints on the roads. Ogadeni refugees have been encouraged to take over the remains of Isaaq shops and houses in what are now ghost towns. Thus, those who were received as refugee guests have supplanted their Isaaq hosts, many of whom - in this bitterly ironic turn of fate - are now refugees in the Ogaden.[11]

Upon their return from refugee camps in Ethiopia, Isaaq elders and the rest of the people were shocked to see that their cities and towns had been reduced to rubble. The main city of Hargeisa was destroyed to a most shocking degree - even the mosques had been bombed from the air and strafed from the ground! The shock and anger influenced the SNM-hosted Popular Congress in Burao (May 1991) which decided to push self-determination beyond federalism to include the right to break the 1960 union and declare the Somaliland Republic.

Unlike in Uganda whose insurrection was led by Yoweri Museveni and his youthful army hiding within Uganda's southern forests, and unlike Liberia at least during the early phase of its revolt, Somalia experienced several armed insurrections divided along clan-family and geographic lines. None of them had a hegemonic leader. Siad's poisoning of clan relations frustrated opposition attempts to form a multi-clan-family based movement. Opposition leaders justified their decentralised clan-family based groupings as the best strategy within the Somali context. Their reasoning echoed the Swahili proverb, 'the medicine for fire is fire' (*dawa ya moto ni moto*). As the armed opposition movements weakened the regime, internal non-violent civilian opposition groups began to be heard. One branch, called the Manifesto Group, consisted of former politicians, senior civil servants and businessmen. A second branch consisted of religious teachers and leaders. Well-known intellectuals signed the declarations distributed by both groups. The Italian and Egyptian governments, with the blessings of the U.S. administration, wanted the Siad regime and the internal non-violent opposition to manage the transition. Obviously, had such moves succeeded, they might have hijacked the transition from the armed opposition movements. The various groups thought that they could bring pressure to bear on the Siad regime, inducing it to manage the transition according to an agreed upon timetable until the transfer of power to a democratically elected government. When this attempt failed and the civil war came close to Mogadishu, the dissident opposition and their foreign backers tried to call a reconciliation conference in Cairo following which elements from the incumbent military dictatorship and the pro-democratic opposition would share executive power temporarily before national elections would be held. This last minute attempt failed as well, and the Siad regime was overthrown following violent uprisings.

A Civil War Run Amok

A few years after Siad took power, political jokes used to circulate in Mogadishu. One of these compared Siad to a novice pilot who decided to fly a plane after reading part one of the flight manual. He did not know how to land the plane, because the instructions were in part two of the manual which he did not have and had not read. Ironically, the insurgents who overthrew the Siad dictatorship and destroyed one of sub-Saharan Africa's largest armies find themselves in a similar dilemma - the civil war seems to continue as if it is running on automatic pilot.

In the north, in the civil war to overthrow Siad which intensified with the SNL assaults of 1988, about 50,000 are estimated to have died and 500,000 flew as refugees into the Haud, in Ethiopia. The total number of displaced persons due to wars was about one million as of early 1991. The USC led effort to defeat Siad in Mogadishu is estimated to have cost 20,000 lives. Recent estimates of the cost of continuation of the civil war in Mogadishu run at 30,000; all this in a nation of roughly four million people in the north, and about six million in the south. Overall, as of December 1991, 4.5 million people remained in serious need of emergency assistance.[12]

Somalia's continuing internal conflict is multi-dimensional and can be explained only by reference to several interrelated factors. These include the relative young age and immaturity of some of the opposition movements - the USC in particular. Formed in 1989, by mid-1990 its armed wing had captured most of central Somalia. When Siad ran out of Mogadishu in late January 1991, one faction of the USC appointed hotel owner Ali Mahdi Mohamed President, thereby alienating the General Aidid branch of the USC, as well as the SNM and the other opposition movements. The USC elected Aidid Chairman of the movement in July 1991, but this move did not lead to reconciliation. Since September 1991, the war continued between Aidid's and Ali Mahdi's clans of the Hawiye clan-family.

The nature of the armed forces facilitates continued conflicts. Both sides head clan militias, 'children armies', who have received no military training, discipline or proper command. There are no logistics or supply units, and as a result the militia use their guns to obtain food and kat (a mild drug chewed in Eastern Africa, especially among the Somalis). As a consequence, even without the raging civil war, the situation borders on anarchy and facilitates banditry. The opposition groups have had no time to forge a common political programme except to overthrow Siad Barre. Cutting across clan lines are conflicts between the new insurgent leaders and old politicians of the parliamentary era, between those who worked under Siad until recently and those who quit his regime much earlier, between civilian leaders and former military officers. The Superpowers have not been involved in the Horn since the demise of the Cold War; however, other powers continue to try to shape political events. Italy, and, in particular, the notorious Ambassador, Mario Sica, has continued to meddle in Somali politics. Sica is reported to have urged Ali Mahdi to go ahead and crown himself before consulting with other USC factions who were outside Mogadishu and abroad. Having failed in the attempt to host a

Cairo reconciliation conference to hijack the transitional process, Italy backed two Djibouti conferences intended to legitimise Ali Mahdi at the expense of the other factions within the USC. The Djibouti conference gave prominence to 'the numerous politicians (including current ministers), who visit Mogadishu from their homes in Europe, Saudi Arabia or the United States, such as ex-Prime Minister Abdirazak Haji Hussein'.[13]

Substantive mediation efforts were attempted through the intervention of clan elders. There are four Hawiye clans, and with two fighting the other two attempted to call several cease-fires and to mediate. One of these, the Hawadle, continued to play a relatively neutral role and to attempt to mediate throughout the period of the conflict. The United Nations imposed a boycott on arms shipments to Somalia; but unfortunately, there were already plenty of arms within Somalia and the Horn. In the south the bloody civil war led eventually to direct international intervention. In April 1992 there was the UN Operation in Somalia (UNOSOM), and when that proved a failure there was the United States-led UN Operation Restore Hope, in December 1992, before in May 1993 responsibility was passed back to the UN Operation for Somalia (UNOSOM II). The effective collapse of the state, with the partial exception of the would-be independent territory of Somaliland, has meant that issues of regionalism are an inevitable aspect of any bottom-up reconstruction of civil society, as well as of local administration.

Meanwhile, the Republic of Somaliland may, if it is able to attain peace, stability and democratic reforms, achieve international recognition. It is also likely that internal and international circumstances may oblige it, in time, to reconsider full independence and opt for some link with Mogadishu in a confederal state. Whatever happens, the independent administration established in former British Somaliland would have served a useful purpose: it has facilitated relief efforts and the renewal of the formerly vital private sector. During my visit to Somaliland in July 1991, I was impressed by the bustling activities of the markets, small shops and private transportation. Relief efforts were conducted mostly by international and indigenous voluntary development organisations. The cities remained devastated, because there was, as yet, no substantial aid necessary to embark on reconstruction. However, with funding from the EEC, Oxfam was rehabilitating the Hargeisa water supply system.

Siad's military brutality and wanton destruction pushed northerners to reclaim their right of self-determination. Nevertheless, north-south contradictions go back to 1960 when the north voluntarily joined the south. The National Assembly gave proportionally excessive advantage to the south. The south monopolised all key posts such as Commander of the Police Forces, Commander of the National Army and so forth. The north thought they would be treated, at least informally, as a 'federal entity'. The south proceeded to take the posts of President, Prime Minister, Minister of Defence, Minister of Interior and Minister of Foreign Affairs. In Somali politics, this is a violation of the rules of consociational politics. The north reacted by voting overwhelmingly against the union constitution in the referendum of 1961. Later on, northern Sandhurst trained officers led by the late Hassan Keid attempted one of Africa's first post-independence coups intended to secede from the south. In the following years, southern domination over the north was felt not only in the political arena but also in the administrative system. Under Siad, this inequality in power-sharing exploded and reached neofascist proportions with Siad treating the majority clan-family in the north, the Isaaq, as if they were aliens or members of a 'caste' that deserves persecution.

The SNM government in the north established a consociationally-derived Cabinet and parliament or National Assembly. It set a two-year period as the transition to prepare a democratic constitution and move towards multi-party elections, though this deadline was not met. A constitution drafting committee headed by Chairman of the Assembly, Ibrahim Meygag Samater, was set up, but progress proved very slow. The judiciary has been separated from the executive and the regions have been granted autonomy. It is not clear at this point whether the regions will be given 'federal status' in the new constitution. Between January 1991 and early 1992, the administration in the north has managed to disarm the urban population and maintain relative stability. Later, however, a small group of former army officers who directed SNM military operations challenged the embryonic government. They were removed from their posts in the Cabinet and administration, and these actions led to conflicts. The confrontation in Burao was mediated by elders, but then some of the dissidents joined others in the port city of Berbera. International NGO's removed their volunteers as tensions mounted. The next few weeks and months were critical for the situation in the north until the more mature SNM and its formally constituted Council of Elders (Guurti) were able to resolve these and other conflicts peacefully.

Conclusion

The issue of federalism was raised in modern Somali history around 1947. To avoid domination the agropastoral Rahanweyn clans inhabiting the southwest parts of ex-Italian Somaliland around the city of Baidoa raised the issue. They lost their bid to attain federal status as Somalia achieved independence as a unitary state. The Siad regime pushed coercion and centralism to levels never experienced before in Somali history. By the 1980s, armed opposition movements rose to combat the Siad military regime. In their documents, they advocated federalism and multi-party democracy. Using clan recruited militias, they waged their wars in a decentralised manner. Unfortunately, Siad's overthrow did not lead to peace and stability. The opposition movements have not shared a common vision and programme, and they lack leaders who are respected and followed by the majority. In the north, the SNM declared independence and began to transmit relief assistance to the war and drought stricken population.

By 1993 it was clear that, with international support, there had to be the pursuit of some more stable political framework as a vital element in Somalia's recovery from years of war and suffering. Whether that framework is eventually for one country (Somalia) or two (Somalia and

Somaliland), it will certainly involve consideration of federal and/or confederal constitutional arrangements.

---

1   Saadia Touval, *Somali Nationalism* (Cambridge: Harvard University Press, 1963), pp. 88 and 106.
2   Mohamed H. Mukhtar, "The Emergence and Role of Political Parties in the Inter-river Region of Somalia from 1946-1960 (Independence)," Annarita Puglielli, editor, *Proceedings of the Third International Congress of Somali Studies* (Roma: Il Pensiero Scientifico Editore, 1988), p. 309.
3   Ibid., p. 310.
4   Ibid., p. 311 and 313.
5   Frantz Fanon, cited in John S. Saul, *The State and Revolution in Eastern Africa* (New York: Monthly Review Press, 1979), p. 409.
8   Ismail Hurreh, SNM Central Committee, "Peace for the Horn of Africa in the Political Program of the SNM," *Proceedings: 4th International Conference on the Horn of Africa May 27-28, 1989*, (New York: Center for the Study of the Horn of Africa, 1990), p. 22. See also pages 19, 20-21 and 23.
9   United Somali Congress (USC) Political Programme cited in Maria Bongartz, op. cit. Appendix 3, point 4.
10 Ibid., Appendix 3, point 12.
11 I. M. Lewis, "The Ogaden and the Fragility of Somali Segmented Nationalism," *Horn of Africa,* Vol. XIII, Numbers 1 and 2, January-March and April-June, 1990,
12 *Horn of Africa Bulletin,* Vol. 3, No. 7, November-December 1991, p. 3.
13 Ibid., p. 9

11 The Economic Dimensions of Federalism in the Horn of Africa

PAUL B HENZE

Though a comparatively new idea in terms of political and economic dialogue in the Horn of Africa, federalism in the sense of decentralised governmental and economic structure can be shown to have a substantial history in the region. In this chapter I propose to illustrate this by looking in turn at the different countries of the Horn, and then to discuss the prospects for the development of federalism in the region as a whole.

The Lessons of Ethiopian History

Ethiopia, next to Egypt the oldest continually existing polity in Africa, has almost always been a relatively decentralised state - at many stages in its long history so decentralised, in fact, that only a vague tradition of statehood, combined with a sense of religious and cultural community, held it together at all. The Ethiopian state was able to survive repeated crises largely because its emperors conceded a high degree of autonomy to the diverse regions and rulers that made up their empire. Much of the time doing so was simply to accept the unavoidable.

On the other hand, notions of autonomy and diversity were an essential feature of the very concept of *yenegusa negast menegist* - a state headed by a king of kings. Kings and subordinate rulers had broad authority in their own territories and often defied the emperor. Regional rulers more often than not wielded more economic power than the king of kings: they regulated trade and markets, imposed duties and taxes, made demands for men and material to maintain armies, and controlled the extraction and distribution of valuable commodities such as metals, salt, ivory, and incense.

With the territorial expansion that came as a result of Menelik's conquests and the concomitant increase in the power of the imperial government, there was little effort to force the entire country into a rigid centralised pattern - either politically or economically. As modernisation steadily accelerated during the long reign of Haile Selassie, a pragmatic balance between the authority of the greatly expanding central government and regional centres of power was maintained. The primary characteristic of Haile Selassie's approach to government was recognition of regional diversity within a broad and steady process of consolidation of the authority - and enhancement of the administrative ability - of the central government. This approach to government was not confined to political matters, but applied to the economic and social spheres of life as well. Though incisively described and analysed by Margery Perham and Christopher Clapham over 40 and 20 years ago, respectively,[1] the nature of Haile Selassie's approach to government can only be fully appreciated by contrasting it to the intrusive, coercive, highly centralising revolutionary regime that attempted to consolidate its hold on the country from 1977 to 1991. In the process of trying to force the entire country into a common political, economic, and social mould, it provoked extremes of fragmentation that may prove difficult to repair. By trying to force the Soviet political and economic model onto the country, it reduced much of it to a condition of stagnation, decline and recurrent famine, like the ex-Soviet Union itself.

The Eritrean Case

The failure of the federation of Eritrea with imperial Ethiopia is currently seen by Eritrean separatists as an example of Haile Selassie's lust to exercise absolute power and a manifestation of the age-old drive of the Amhara to dominate all other Ethiopian peoples. These interpretations are oversimplified and self-serving. Eritrea, unlike most long established traditional regions of the country, was an ethnically and geographically diverse border region which had no comprehensive political identity before it became an Italian colony at the end of the 19th century. Though Italian colonialism gave it a substantial degree of economic coherence,[2] the territory still lacked internal political, religious, and ethnic cohesion when the federation came into being in 1952. The Eritrean population continues to be characterised by great ethnic, linguistic, and religious diversity.

The fact that federation with Ethiopia did not endure can be attributed to several causes: (1) the Addis Ababa government had little ability and limited incentive to create a genuine federal government structure, and it was not pressed to do so by the international community that had sponsored the federation; (2) the international situation in the Red Sea region gave Haile Selassie justified cause for worry about radical Arab exploitation of dissidence in Eritrea; and last, but perhaps most important of all (3) Eritreans remained politically divided and developed no sense of common purpose as a regional entity within the Ethiopian state - i.e., they failed to exploit and protect their special political status as a federated territory.

It remains to be seen whether the intense guerrilla struggle of the past years has created a sense of common purpose sufficient to sustain either independence or effective existence within a new Ethiopian federation in the future. Eritrea's economic potential remains high but can best be realised only within the framework of a federation or confederational arrangement with the rest of Ethiopia and a common market encompassing the entire Horn-Red Sea region.[3]

Sudan, Somalia, and Djibouti

Sudan and Somalia became states only as a result of the initiatives of colonial powers. From every point of view - political, economic, cultural, religious, and ethnic - Sudan remains an agglomeration of regions that retain their distinctive character. Misguided efforts by successive independent governments to administer the country in centralised fashion have strengthened regionalism to the point where the country is confronted with the prospect of semi-permanent fragmentation.

Somalis, united in language, culture, religion, and way of life, developed no centralised political structure until they were de-colonised. The colonial experience resulted, in part, in new regionalisms superimposed upon pre-existing clan structures. In its pristine pastoral democratic form, Somalia can perhaps be regarded as a primitive form of federation. More than two decades of Siad Barre's centralising authoritarianism has produced a disastrous situation where Somalis' only hope for political survival as a state appears to be in transformation from a *de facto* to a *de jure* federation.

The Republic of Djibouti is unique in the Horn as the colonial combination of two traditionally hostile peoples: Afars and Issas. It has withstood more than a decade of independence with its state structure strengthened - in contrast to all other Horn countries. The strains of conflict among its two neighbours have contributed to the consolidation of Djibouti's statehood. Economically, Djibouti functions as the hub of an informal East African free trade area. It thus stands as a hopeful element for the future of the entire troubled area of which it forms a part. The fact that it was chosen as the seat of the Intergovernmental Authority on Drought and Development (IGADD) is of more than symbolic importance, for this organisation is the product of regional initiative and has attained a certain degree of independent existence that offers promise for the future.

Present Economic Conditions in the Horn

Djibouti is a good place to begin discussion of the present economic condition of the Horn because it is the only Horn country that has maintained a relatively open and viable economy—in spite of the fact that it has only a few acres of cultivable land, no major mineral resources, almost no fresh water, and an extremely inhospitable climate. Its advantages include geography and a predictable degree of political stability - ensured, to be sure, by the presence of a modest French military force which makes a positive contribution to its economy. Djibouti has become an entrepot through which all manner of goods, some legally and much illegally from the point of view of one or more of the political jurisdictions involved, flow in and out. Goods transiting Djibouti have helped keep northern Somalia and eastern Ethiopia supplied with both necessities and luxuries, the ultimate origins of which are often Hong Kong, Japan, and South Korea. In the process, old caravan routes to the Ethiopian highlands, dormant since the 19th century, took on a new life.

As governments in the three major Horn countries became bogged down in increasingly futile military efforts to subdue portions of their territory and as their efforts to establish centralised control over their economies faltered, economic relationships throughout the region increasingly escaped government control and took on a life of their own. Complex political and economic factors lie behind these developments, which are by no means uniform from one Horn state to another.[4] The results have been much the same throughout the region, however. The underground or unofficial economy, as it is variously called, has increasingly become the *real* economy.

Patterns of economic exchange do not reflect lines of government political authority or military control within countries, though economic exchanges are inevitably affected by severe hostilities and large movements of refugees. In Eritrea the flow of goods between government - and insurgent - held areas never ceased. Patterns of economic exchange between countries seldom reflect the state of formal relations on the governmental plane. Strained relations between Ethiopia and Somalia and between Ethiopia and Sudan have not disrupted informal trade across borders. Goods are not only bartered - in fact, they appear only seldom to be bartered. Money is exchanged. The two strongest currencies in the Horn are, not surprisingly, the U.S. dollar - but more surprisingly indeed, the Ethiopian birr. The astute financial management which was characteristic of imperial Ethiopia persisted through all the vicissitudes of the revolutionary period. Though currently overvalued in terms of the dollar by 400% or more, the Ethiopian birr has retained the distinction of being one of the few Third World currencies that escaped inflationary collapse during the 1980s.[5]

None of this is to say that the economic condition of the Horn is good. It is not as bad as official statistics often make it appear to be. But for the most part Horn societies have only survived economically. Development and modernisation on a major scale, with medium - and long-range goals defined and agreed upon, have almost ceased. Before taking power in Ethiopia, insurgent movements claimed to have created conditions for self-propelled development in regions they controlled. Their accomplishments, though admirable, were nevertheless extremely modest. The SPLA makes no such claims. Some parts of Somalia that have escaped from Mogadishu's control enjoy a limited degree of prosperity from export of livestock, a trade flow which is in part fed from Ethiopia.

Everywhere the emphasis has been on short-term activity, quick profit, and satisfaction of urgent needs. The fact that so many entrepreneurs are willing to take the risks of operating in illegal or semi-legal circumstances offers hope for the future economic development of the Horn, but until political conditions are stabilised and favourable, such men cannot realise their full potential for generating economic momentum. Only a few institutions such as Ethiopian Airlines were able to survive the debilitating effects of bad government and plan coherently for future economic expansion.

The main effect of economic adjustments decreed in Ethiopia in 1990 was to bring to the surface and legalise activity that was already taking place. New investment and initiative were small in scale even after the fall of the Derg. An economic upsurge is foreseeable in Ethiopia as well as Eritrea if the new administrations develop coherent economic policies.

The Inevitability of Political Federalism in the Horn

Internal political federalism is the only solution for maintenance of the major Horn states as viable members of the international community. The authoritarian, coercive centralised approach to government in the Horn has failed. Reconstituted Horn governments must gain acceptance by providing services to the component parts of their countries. They cannot expect to impose their will by force. No Horn country can maintain an effective military establishment on the basis of internally generated resources. No foreign power is going to be willing in the future to supply the kind of military aid the Soviet Union and, to a much lesser degree, other foreign powers have provided over the past three decades. An international moratorium on all arms for the Horn is going to come close to realisation in fact, whether formally proclaimed or not.

Africa to a higher degree than other parts of the Third World has suffered from overemphasis on politics to the detriment of economics. In more acute form than most of their African counterparts, Horn leaders of the 1970s and 1980s militarised politics and bureaucratised economics. In the process, they saddled themselves with economic and social dogma that stymied development and modernisation and caused their societies to turn in upon themselves. To break the vicious downward spiral of political, economic, and social degeneration, future Horn leaders will be successful in maintaining themselves and leading their countries to recovery only if they adopt a radically different approach to politics from that which has been fashionable in the recent past. They must emphasise national reconciliation and recovery based on consensus about a limited range of central government functions. They must abandon military coercion. They must emphasise economics over politics, where necessary postponing political debates and decisions for the future while they exert themselves to create economic momentum. Economic momentum has the best chance of becoming self-sustaining when individuals and private groups are given maximum economic freedom.[6] Private enterprise and free markets are inherent features of the informal economy that exists throughout theHorn. Future governments will have no alternative to giving disaffected regions both political and economic autonomy—leaving disaffected populations and leaders to take a high degree of responsibility for generating economic momentum in their regions. Only in Ethiopia since the fall of the Derg at the end of May 1991 have these positive trends begun to be observable.

The Economic Dimensions of Federalism

The basis for economic federalism already exists in many forms and past experience - e.g., many of the regional economic development projects that have operated successfully in all Horn countries - offers many pertinent lessons. To the extent that societies in the Horn are functioning economically, they are doing so on the basis of ad hoc federalism. This reality needs to be recognised by future governments and built upon. Insurgent movements which managed to sustain development efforts in the regions under their control can expand them and should be encouraged to rationalise them by avoiding overcentralisation and bureaucratisation. The potential for economic development in many parts of the Horn is so great that economic activity can take place in parallel at different administrative levels without serious conflict of interests. While governments will be well advised to encourage and rely on private initiative, there should also be room for many different ownership and management approaches, including co-operatives and continuation of autonomous state economic enterprises and development authorities, some of which have a good record.

National governments will have more than enough to do to ensure the provision of services that only they can oversee effectively: highways, railways, communications, currency and banking, public health, education and training, meteorological services, and other such arrangements that modern economies require. But national governments need no monopoly and should not inhibit regional and private initiative in any of these functional areas. National governments will also need to continue to conduct diplomacy, manage bilateral economic arrangements, and maintain relations with international development organisations, lending institutions, and regulatory agencies. Every Horn country belongs to numerous international organisations and benefits from agreements that affect its economy by entitlement to grants, loans, and technical assistance, provision of services, customs exemptions, and education and training opportunities.

Central planners in the Horn have tended to operate as economic dictators, remote from the economic realities of their countries. In developing countries, planners almost always have an inherent tendency to favour autarkic arrangements and display bias against private enterprise. In practice in the Horn, planning bodies have as often inhibited economic initiative as encouraged it. Central planning commissions should be sharply reduced in size and transformed into research groups which engage in evaluation, research, and estimation of long-range needs for infrastructure and services. They should be deprived of administrative and executive authority.

Economic federalism is a principle that can be beneficially applied between, as well as within, countries and across international borders between regions of countries without need for central government intervention. This, too, is what has already been happening throughout the Horn. Rather than inhibit it, future Horn governments should encourage these relationships and exploit existing regional economic interchanges as a basis for broader co-operation between states. Horn economies, it is true, are in many respects actually or potentially competitive in terms of the meagre range of primary products that make up the list of their declining exports: grains, pulses, vegetables, coffee, live animals, hides and skins, and animal and vegetable fibres. This should not be the end of the story, however.

The potential of all Horn countries to develop new primary crops[7] and process both traditional and new agricultural products for local consumption and export is great. Mineral exploitation may prove to be a rewarding field for expansion. In many instances the potential of new economic initiatives can be realised more rapidly if countries co-operate, share knowledge, services and develop joint processing facilities. The Horn as a whole is currently an energy deficit region. Its water power resources are barely tapped. Known petroleum and gas deposits are not being exploited because of unfavourable security conditions and economic stagnation. Once serious development of energy resources in the Horn begins, horizons for co-operative arrangements that will benefit all countries appear unlimited.

---

[1] Perham, Margery, *The Government Of Ethiopia*, London, Faber and Faber, 1948; Christopher Clapham, *Haile Selassie's Government*, London, Longmans, 1969.

[2] The significance of the Italian colonial economic legacy is demonstrated, sometimes inadvertently, by the continuing debate about its value. See, e.g., Araia Tseggai, 'Historical Analysis of Infrastructural Development in Italian Eritrea: 1885-1941' in two parts in *Journal of Eritrean Studies* (Grambling, La.), Nos. 1 & 2, 1986 & 1987.

[3] I developed this thesis at length in 'Eritrea - the Economic Challenge,' another essay in this volume.

[4] For a more extensive discussion see Christopher Clapham, 'The Political Economy of Conflict in the Horn of Africa,' in *Survival*, September/October 1990, pp 403-419.

[5] The official rate as of time of writing remained 2.07/$1, though the street rate in Addis Ababa in late 1991 was eight birr to the dollar.

[6] The arguments, still heard among Africanists more often than from Africans themselves, that "human needs" ought to be given absolute priority over considerations of macro-economic development, that private enterprise and free markets enrich the few and push the majority deeper into poverty, that grants of aid from governments and international organisations are preferable to foreign investment, and that only the state can ensure the welfare of the masses are all contradicted by the experience of the past three decades. Human needs cannot long be met at the expense of economic development or satisfied by endless reliance on international charity. Only expanding productivity and generation of capital can provide the basis for permanent improvement in conditions of life.

[7] E.g., Vernonia galamensis.